GALLUP
YOUTH
SURVEY:

MAJOR ISSUES AND TRENDS

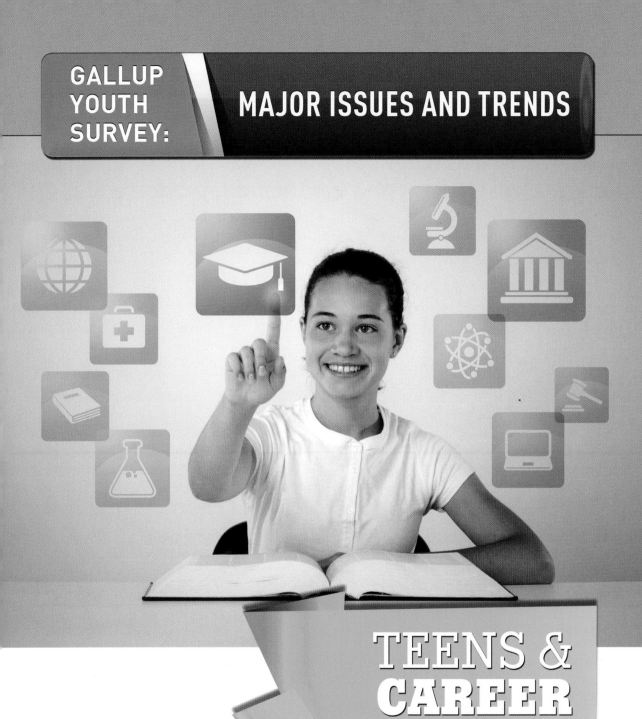

TEENS &
CAREER
CHOICES

Hal Marcovitz

**Developed in
Association with the
Gallup Organization**

TEENS &
CAREER
CHOICES

Hal Marcovitz

**Developed in
Association with the
Gallup Organization**

Mason Crest
450 Parkway Drive, Suite D
Broomall, PA 19008
www.masoncrest.com

Printed and bound in the United States of America.

CPSIA Compliance Information: Batch #GYS2013. For further information, contact Mason Crest at 1-866-MCP-Book

First printing
1 3 5 7 9 8 6 4 2

Library of Congress Cataloging-in-Publication Data

Marcovitz, Hal.
 Teens and career choices / Hal Marcovitz.
     pages cm. — (The Gallup youth survey : major issues and trends)
 Includes bibliographical references and index.
 Audience: Grade 7 to 8.
 ISBN 978-1-4222-2950-7 (hc) — ISBN 978-1-4222-8867-2 (ebook)
 1. Vocational guidance—United States—Juvenile literature. 2. Teenagers—
Vocational guidance—United States—Juvenile literature. 3. High school
students—Vocational guidance—United States—Juvenile literature.
 4. Teenagers—Employment—United States—Juvenile literature. I. Title.
 HF5382.5.U5M357 2014
 331.7020835'0973—dc23
                                    2013007179

The Gallup Youth Survey: Major Issues and Trends series ISBN: 978-1-4222-2948-4

Contents

Introduction

By George Gallup

A s the United States moves into the new century, there is a vital need for insight into what it means to be a young person in America. Today's teenagers will be the leaders and shapers of the 21st century. The future direction of the United States is being determined now in their hearts and minds and actions. Yet how much do we as a society know about this important segment of the U.S. populace who have the potential to lift our nation to new levels of achievement and social health?

We need to hear the voices of young people, and to help them better articulate their fears and their hopes. Our youth have much to share with their elders—is the older generation really listening? Is it carefully monitoring the hopes and fears of teenagers today? Failure to do so could result in severe social consequences.

The Gallup Youth Survey was conducted between 1977 and 2006 to help society meet this responsibility to youth, as well as to inform and guide our leaders by probing the social and economic attitudes and behaviors of young people. With theories abounding about the views, lifestyles, and values of adolescents, the Gallup Youth Survey, through regular scientific measurements of teens themselves, served as a sort of reality check.

Surveys reveal that the image of teens in the United States today is a negative one. Teens are frequently maligned, misunderstood, or simply ignored by their elders. Yet over four decades the Gallup Youth Survey provided ample evidence of the very special qualities of the nation's youngsters. In fact, if our society is less racist, less sexist, less polluted, and more peace loving, we can in considerable measure thank our young people, who have been on the leading edge on these issues. And the younger generation is not geared to greed: survey after survey has shown that teens have a keen interest in helping those people, especially in their own communities, who are less fortunate than themselves

Young people have told Gallup that they are enthusiastic about helping others, and are willing to work for world peace and a healthy world. They feel positive about their schools and even more positive about their teachers. A large majority of American teenagers have reported that they are happy and excited about the future, feel very close to their families, are likely to marry, want to have children, are satisfied with their personal lives, and desire to reach the top of their chosen careers.

But young adults face many threats, so parents, guardians, and concerned adults must commit themselves to do everything possible to help tomorrow's parents, citizens, and leaders avoid or overcome risky behaviors so that they can move into the future with greater hope and understanding.

The Gallup Organization is enthusiastic about this partnership with Mason Crest Publishers. Through carefully and clearly written books on a variety of vital topics dealing with teens, Gallup Youth Survey statistics are presented in a way that gives new depth and meaning to the data. The focus of these books is a practical one—to provide readers with the statistics and solid information that they need to understand and to deal with each important topic.

— — —

It is disheartening that surveys show between one-third and one-half of adults in the U. S. workforce would choose a different kind of work if they had the chance to start their working life again. Perhaps a reason for this is that young people who are about to enter their working lives are often not aware of the options, and also may not recognize their own special strengths and gifts that they can bring to a job or profession. This book is important because it can open the minds of readers to job possibilities and prospects. It provides information on how to apply for jobs and to make the best impression. It explores the military as one option, as well as nonprofit organizations. The book is filled with helpful advice for both those who want to reflect upon a future career, and those who are about to actively seek a job.

A lot is at stake in career choices—not only the well-being and mental health of individuals, but the vitality and productivity of society as a whole. I hope this book will find its way into the hands not only of young people, but also guidance counselors and others who steer young people toward fulfilling lives.

Chapter One

Two students take notes while a doctor performs brain surgery in a Los Angeles hospital. Today many schools offer programs that help young people decide what kind of career they would like to pursue after graduation.

A New Generation of Workers

Katie Rupert, Ashley Dominick, and other students at Howell High School in Howell, Michigan, were able to get a jump-start on their ambitions to become health-care professionals. Their school offered a course in medical occupations, which enabled the students to find out what being a nurse or paramedic or physician is all about. Their teacher, Darlene Smith, is a registered nurse, and the Howell students were able to receive more than just classroom instruction. As part of the course, the students were assigned to work with real medical professionals at Howell-area health-care institutions.

Shortly after enrolling in the health occupations course, the students found themselves on the job at Medilodge, a Howell elder-care facility. "I knew we would learn a lot of things to do for patients," Ashley, then 17, told a reporter for the *Detroit News*. "I like it. It's fun. You have more of a one-on-one with people." Ashley told the reporter that after high school she hopes to attend college, study radiology, and start a career as a magnetic resonance imaging technician.

Students in Howell High School's health occupations class learn skills they would need if they wanted to become full-time health-care workers. For example, the students are taught the Heimlich maneuver; how to take vital signs; how to assist burned, bleeding, or unconscious patients; cardiopulmonary resuscitation and other first-aid techniques; and how to provide personal care, such as bathing, shaving, oral hygiene, and nail care. These experiences look very good on the résumé of someone interested in a career in the field. Katie, 17, told the *Detroit News* that she enrolled because second-year health occupations students are qualified to take a state examination to become certified nursing assistants. With the certification, Katie could hold a job in a hospital, nursing home, clinic, or similar medical center while she worked toward a college degree as a registered nurse. "My goal is to become a registered nurse," she said. "Getting an assistant nurse certificate is part of my plan."

Katie Rupert and Ashley Dominick are not unique among today's high school students. Across the United States, millions of young people have made career plans, and they begin doing something about them long before they graduate from high school. Some students, like Katie and Ashley, are lucky enough to attend schools that steer their students toward career guidance. In many cases, students base their college searches on which schools they think will be best able to prepare them for the careers they want to pursue. Students with no interest in college are often able to receive career training through vocational-educational programs, where they can learn a trade such as plumbing, carpentry, or cosmetology.

What Jobs do Teens Want?

The Gallup Organization, a national polling firm, has often studied how teens view their career choices through the Gallup Youth Survey, a longtime project by the firm to assess the views of young people in the United States. In 2003, the Gallup Youth Survey asked 1,200 young people between the ages of 13 and 17 to name their top career choices. The top selection was doctor, nurse, or similar medical professional, which was chosen by 10 percent of all teens. This was followed by teacher (8 percent), computer professional (6 percent), athlete (5 percent), lawyer (4 percent), veterinarian (4 percent), engineer (3 percent), chef (3 percent), musician (3 percent), member of the military (3 percent), and mechanic (2 percent).

When broken down by gender, the answers are not quite the same, meaning that boys and girls often have vastly different ideas of where they think their career paths will take them.

According to the answers given only by the boys, the top career pick in the Gallup Youth Survey was computer professional (9 percent), followed by athlete (8 percent), doctor or medical professional (6 percent), engineer (6 percent), mechanic (4 percent), member of the military (4 percent), teacher (4 percent), lawyer (3 percent), chef (3 percent), law enforcement officer (2 percent), and musician (2 percent).

On the other hand, 13 percent of girls made teaching their top career choice, followed by doctor or medical professional (11 percent), veterinarian (8 percent), lawyer (6 percent), nurse (5 percent), musician (3 percent), chef (3 percent), actor (2 percent), psychologist (2 percent), scientist (2 percent), and athlete (2 percent).

Some of these career choices are less realistic than others. For example, although a relatively large percentage of young men

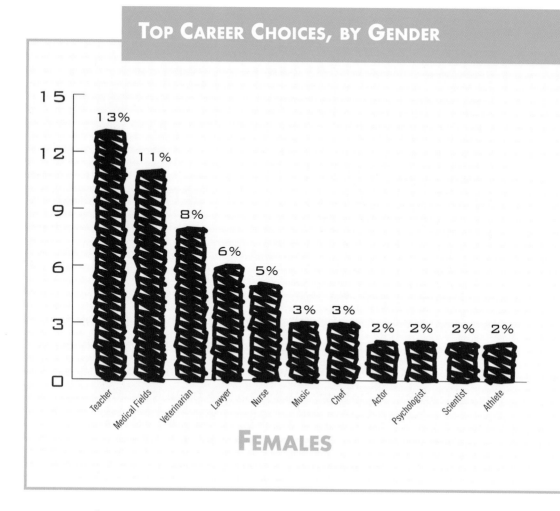

FEMALES

want to become professional athletes—drawn to this dream, undoubtedly, by the astronomical salaries as well as the fame that goes along with the job—very few athletes have what it takes to make it in pro sports. But in most cases, there will be job opportunities awaiting today's middle-school and high-school students as they enter the U.S. workforce.

Predicting future economic trends is hardly a foolproof science. Many unforeseen factors can occur that could cause economic downturns, such as war, energy shortages, and scandals that force major employers to stop hiring, lay off workers, or even go out of business. Still, the U.S. Bureau of Labor Statistics, the federal

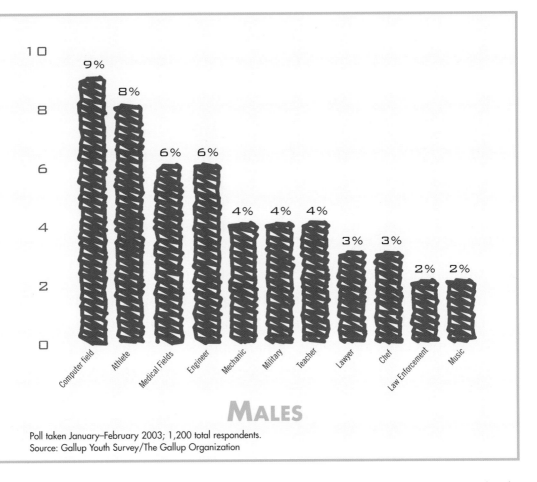

10

9%

8

8%

6

6% 6%

4

4% 4% 4%

3% 3%

2

2% 2%

0

Computer field Athlete Medical Fields Engineer Mechanic Military Teacher Lawyer Chef Law Enforcement Music

MALES

Poll taken January–February 2003; 1,200 total respondents.
Source: Gallup Youth Survey/The Gallup Organization

agency that tracks job growth and trends, anticipates that today's young people will find the economy healthy and jobs plentiful by the time they are ready to join the working world. "Industries and occupations related to health care, personal care and social assistance, and construction are projected to have the fastest job growth between 2010 and 2020," the U.S. Bureau of Labor Statistics reported in February 2012. "Total employment is projected to grow by 14.3 percent over the decade, resulting in 20.5 million new jobs."

The Bureau of Labor Statistics predicted that in 2020, the unemployment rate will be around 5 percent, which means that virtually anybody who wants to work and contribute as a productive citizen, according to the bureau's projections, jobs should be available.

Today's teens do hope to contribute to society as productive workers, according to the Gallup Youth Survey. In a poll released in January 2004, the Gallup Organization reported that career-oriented goals were important to most young people. The survey asked the question, "What would you say are your goals in life?" A total of 71 percent of the 517 respondents said their top goal is to finish high school and attend college or another post-secondary educational program, while 53 percent of the respondents said finding a good job or career is important to them. In addition, 13 percent said being "successful" or "famous" is an important goal, while 12 percent said being "financially secure" or "rich" are important goals. Certainly, being successful and financially secure are natural outcomes of a good career.

What Jobs Will Be Available?

A 2012 Bureau of Labor Statistics report looked at who will be working in 2020, and determined that students who are in middle school and high school today will make up a large share of the workforce by 2020. The federal agency projected that by 2020, there will be some 18.3 million people between the ages of 16 and 24 in the workforce. This represents 11.1 percent of the total American workforce.

By 2020, the so-called "baby-boom generation" will have moved entirely into the 55-years-and-older age group. The "baby-boomers" are people born during the two decades after the end of World War II, between 1946 and 1964. They represented the largest generations of Americans to hit the labor force. By 2020, workers 55 years and older will make up 25.2 percent of the labor force. As the baby boomers retire, their jobs will be filled by the next generation of workers between the ages of 25 and 54. This category of workers is considered to be of "prime working age." According to the Bureau of Labor Statistics, workers between the ages of 25 and 54 will make up 63.7 percent of the 2020 labor force.

The key question for most young people is, which careers hold the most promise for the next generation of workers, and which hold the least promise? The U.S. Bureau of Labor Statistics attempted to answer both those questions in a 2012 report. The agency identified the occupations that are projected to offer the most chances for employment in the decade leading up to the year

Young people wait in line at a job fair in New York. The U.S. Bureau of Labor Statistics estimates that by the year 2020 the unemployment rate will be fairly stable, meaning that many different jobs will be available.

2020, as well as the occupations where employment growth is least likely.

As for the jobs with most potential for growth, the Bureau of Labor Statistics reported that in each case, those 20 occupations will account for more than 52 percent of the new jobs that will become available by 2020.

It should come as no surprise that many of the jobs will be centered in the health-care industry. As baby-boomers grow older, they will need more medical care and, therefore, more people will be needed to provide that care. In fact, the bureau said, medical-related professions will account for seven of the 20 fastest-growing occupational categoriess. They include personal and home care aides, medical assistants, physicians' assistants, medical records and health information technicians, home health aides, physical therapist aides, occupational therapist aides, physical therapist assistants, audiologists, occupational therapist assistants, speech-language pathologists, dental assistants, dental hygienists, pharmacy technicians, social and human service assistants, fitness trainers and aerobics instructors, and mental health and substance abuse social workers.

Some of those jobs seem to be virtually the same. What is the difference, for example, between a physical therapist aide and a physical therapist assistant? According to the Bureau of Labor Statistics, they perform different duties and require different levels of education. A physical therapist assistant will help the patient exercise or may provide massage to the patient's injury. The assistant may also apply hot and cold packs to the injury and help the therapist perform other treatments. An aide works under the supervision of the therapist and the assistant. The aide cleans the therapy area and may help transport patients by pushing wheelchairs or helping them walk by physically supporting them. The aide may also perform clerical tasks, such as ordering supplies, answering the phone and filing paperwork. A physical therapist assistant needs an associate degree from a college while a physical therapist aide needs only a high school education and brief period of on-the-job training.

The next largest group of most-desired workers will be in the computer field. That should come as no surprise, either. With technology constantly changing, more and more people will be needed to keep up with the advancements in the information industry. According to the Bureau of Labor Statistics, five of the most-needed occupational categories will be in computer-related fields. They include applications software engineers, systems software engineers, computer support specialists, network administrators, network systems analysts, computer systems analysts, desktop publishers, database administrators, information systems man-

Young people with an interest in medicine as a career will be in a good position when they finish school, because there will likely be a great demand for workers in fields related to science and health care.

agers, and computer research scientists.

Rounding out the top most-needed occupational categories are veterinary assistants and laboratory animal caretakers, veterinary technologists and technicians, food-service workers, and special-education teachers.

According to the Bureau of Labor Statistics, in 2020 there will be fewer jobs for farm or ranch workers, order clerks, bank tellers, insurance claims clerks, word processors and typists, sewing machine operators, dishwashers, switchboard operators, loan interviewers and clerks. Also, the bureau said, fewer jobs will be available for electrical and electronic equipment assemblers, machine feeders, telephone operators, secretaries (except in the legal, medical, and executive fields), prepress technicians and workers, office machine operators, and cutting, punching, and press machine operators. Rounding out the least-desirable professions, the bureau recommended that young people should not look for jobs as post office clerks, railroad brake and switch operators, wholesale and retail buyers, meter readers, butchers and meat cutters, parts salespersons, inspectors and testers, government program interviewers, door to door sales workers, purchasing clerks, railroad conductors and yardmasters, and barbers.

Although in recent years some companies have outsourced computer programming positions to companies in India and other Asian countries, the computer field is still expected to be a large part of the job market in the next five to ten years.

In 2013, three-quarters of U.S. adults expected to have to continue working past retirement age.

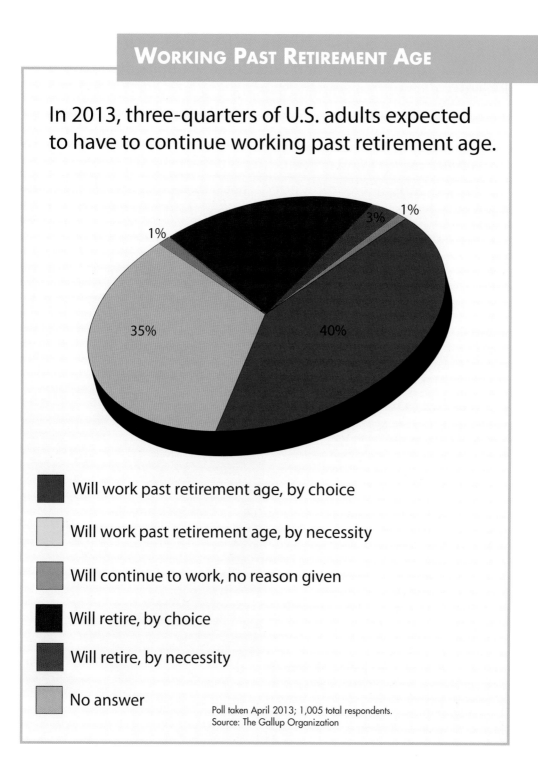

Poll taken April 2013; 1,005 total respondents.
Source: The Gallup Organization

Young people who get serious about their future while still in high school know that to land a good job in a rewarding career, it will take hard work, talent, and motivation, Many will also need training after they receive their high school diplomas. The students in the Howell High School health occupations class are aware of what it will take to get to where they want to go. One of the class members, 16-year-old Shawna Butte, said she enrolled in the health occupations class specifically to explore a future career. "I thought if I took the class it would help me decide what career I'd want to succeed in," she told a newspaper reporter. "It's a good class because you learn a lot and get to meet new people. Here at Medilodge you get to meet the patients and the workers. You get to meet with them and see what their jobs are. It's a good thing to help you in life."

Chapter Two

Many young people find their first jobs in service industries, such as restaurants. These types of jobs are good for teenagers because they give them an opportunity to earn money and gain work experience.

Balancing Work and Study

Laura Curtin, a 17-year-old student at Beechwood High School in Fort Mitchell, Kentucky, worked up to 25 hours a week at a local pharmacy. Usually, she arrived at the pharmacy at 3:30 P.M. and worked until 9 P.M. Laura told a reporter for the *Cincinnati Enquirer* that she had to put in those hours to pay for her car insurance. Even though she logged long hours in her after-school job, Laura managed to maintain her A average. "Sometimes [work] does get in the way," Laura acknowledged to the reporter. "Getting schoolwork done can be a balancing act of late nights and pre-planning."

Although Laura seemed to be able to handle the responsibilities of going to school while holding down a part-time job, Dr. Fred Bassett, the superintendent of the Beechwood Independent School District, was not sure that working and studying are compatible for most students. He told the *Cincinnati Enquirer*, "If students try to work too

COMMON JOBS FOR TEENAGERS

Which of these jobs have you or one of your friends held?

Job	Percentage
Babysitting	76%
Cutting grass	68%
Fast-food restaurant	46%
Bagging groceries	46%
Shoveling snow	42%
Full service restaurant	41%
Working on cars	34%
Day-care center	33%
Walking dogs	32%
Cleaning garages or basements	25%
Bicycle shop	13%
Other jobs	38%

Poll taken March–June 1997; 503 total respondents.
Source: Gallup Youth Survey; The Gallup Organization

many hours, do too many extracurricular activities and study, something's going to suffer."

According to the U.S. Bureau of Labor Statistics, 20.9 million people between the ages of 16 and 24 held jobs in 2010. Many people believe that employment offers valuable experience to teenagers. They learn about responsibility and workplace etiquette, discover new skills, and find themselves managing their own money, probably for the first time in their lives. Other educators, like Dr. Bassett, are not sure that teenagers facing rigorous course loads at school should be working. A 1998 report by the National Academy of Sciences found that students under the age of 18 who worked more than 20 hours a week didn't do as well in school as students who did not work. The study determined that working students slept less, studied less, and made less time for exercise. The academy also found that working students were more likely to use drugs.

More recently, a 2011 study conducted at the University of Michigan found that young people who worked 20 hours a week or more while they were high school were less likely to complete college than students who worked 15 hours or less a week. More than half of the students who worked less completed college by the time they were 30 years old, compared to just 36 percent of those who worked 25 hours per week and 20 percent of those who worked more than 30 hours per week.

On the other hand, some studies have found different results. In 2003, University of Minnesota sociologist Jeylan Mortimer released the results of a long-term study in which she followed the lives of 750 St. Paul residents over a 12-year period, beginning in their high school years and ending when they were in their mid-20s. Mortimer found that study participants who worked in part-time jobs as students went on to have better time-management skills, better academic records in college, and were able to have more options for full-time employment than the participants who did not work in high school. She found that the part-time workers learned skills that they were able to put to use in their careers, such as how to deal with work-related stress. Mortimer's study also contradicted the long-held notion that schoolwork suffers when the student holds a part-time job.

The Gallup Youth Survey found that about 34 percent of teenagers hold wage-paying after-school jobs when it polled young people on the issue in 1997. In interviews with 503 young people between the ages of 13 and 17, the Gallup Organization determined that 20 percent hold jobs on school nights and weekends, 11 percent work on weekends only, and 3 percent of young people work on weeknights only. According to the poll, 55 percent of the teens work between four and six hours on school nights, while 38 percent work between one and three hours on school nights. Just 7 percent of the respondents said they work between seven and nine hours on school nights. Of the teenagers who said they work on school nights, 14 percent said they are "almost always" or "often" tired during class because of their after-school jobs.

Similar Gallup Youth Surveys have also supported the notion that part-time jobs wear down teenagers. In 1997, 69 percent of teenagers responding to a Gallup Youth Survey reported that they feel tired in school, giving as their reasons late-night television watching but also after-school jobs. A year later, 272 teenagers high-achieving teens were also asked by the Gallup Youth Survey to describe how they feel in school, and 68 percent of those young people reported feeling tired as well. Finally, in 1997, the Gallup Youth Survey asked 491 young people between the ages of 13 and 17 to list the activities that occupy them after school; 43 percent responded that they work at a job. When asked how often that activity as well as similar activities get in the way of their home-work, 14 percent said "almost always," 16 percent said "often," and 29 percent said "sometimes."

Jobs Available to Young People

Even if the young employee is only cleaning tables in a fast-food restaurant, researchers suggest that the job will give that worker an understanding of responsibility and a degree of independence while providing him or her with money that the employee may need for college. Those were the conclusions reached in a report issued by the New York-based Families and Work Institute, a non-profit center that researches labor-related issues.

The study, titled "Youth and Employment," found that 78 percent of high school students work in paid or unpaid jobs during the school year or summer. The survey found that girls and boys tended to work in different types of jobs. Girls gravitated toward jobs that included babysitting or caring for elderly people. They also worked in hospitals or other health-care facilities, or found jobs as tutors, camp counselors, lifeguards, or coaches. The study found that only 7 percent of boys performed those types of jobs. Meanwhile, most boys gravitated toward jobs that included some type of physical labor. They found jobs as landscapers or farm laborers, or worked on construction sites, in factories, or perform-ing non-sales work for large retail stores (such as on the loading

Even the simplest jobs, such as dog walking or babysitting, teach young people about responsibility.

docks), or in warehouses. Only 4 percent of girls found jobs in those areas, the study said.

Whatever wages they earned, the study found that students were surprisingly good savers. Ninety-three percent of the teenage workers said they put at least part of their wages aside for the future. Fifty-nine percent of the students who participated in the study said they needed to save money for college or a similar purpose, while 16 percent of the workers said they needed part-time employment to help out with family finances.

APPLYING FOR A JOB

For many teenagers, their first job will likely be filling orders in a fast-food restaurant, punching a cash register in a convenience store, or supervising young children at a summer camp. Those jobs can be fairly easy to find, as long as the applicant knows how to apply.

Experts on teen employment say it generally is not necessary for a teenager to wear a suit and tie or prepare a résumé in order to apply for most part-time or summer jobs. After all, camp counselors aren't required to wear suits while standing lifeguard duty at the pool. Still, Cindy Pervola and Debby Hobgood, authors of the book *How to Get a Job if You're a Teenager*, advise young job applicants to dress neatly. "Pants and a button down shirt work well (girls could wear a skirt instead of pants), or even a pair of jeans is OK as long as they aren't old and worn and the place of business is casual," wrote the authors, both of whom are experienced youth counselors.

Also, while the authors advise that it probably will not be necessary for a young person to draft a résumé, there are certain facts all teens looking for work should have at their fingertips while filling out job applications. Those facts include the person's Social Security number; names, addresses, and telephone numbers of schools attended; information about previous employers, if any; and a list of at least three people who agree to act as references, along with their

Student workers also tend to look ahead. The Families and Work Institute reported in the study that 82 percent of teenage employees expected to graduate from a four-year college, and most of them said they hope to obtain fulfilling careers. "The vast majority of students want to find jobs that are personally meaningful to them (84 percent), to work with people who treat them well (78 percent) and to have jobs where they can be creative and use their skills (69 percent)," said the Families and Work Institute study.

Students have a good idea of what their future employers will be looking for in employees. A total of 75 percent of the students who participated in the study said an employer wants to hire

addresses and phone numbers. The applicant should also have a firm idea of when he or she would be available to start work, and the hours each week he or she is willing to devote to the job.

If an applicant feels he or she needs a résumé, Pervola and Hobgood advise that the document be typed neatly, and include the following information: name, address, and phone number of the applicant; educational background, listing all schools attended; work experience, including dates previous jobs were held; personal interests and areas of expertise, such as musical, artistic, or athletic talents; awards or other forms of recognition; and any other information about the applicant that might enhance his or her value to the organization. For example, a young person applying for office work may want to cite the software programs with which he is familiar. An applicant for a job at a summer camp would want to note that she helped supervise elementary school children during a class in family and consumer science.

"Brag about yourself," Pervola and Hobgood advise. "List sports, clubs and other activities in which you participate, languages you speak fluently, special training you have received. . . . Leave nothing out, no matter how insignificant you think it might be. It says a lot about who you are."

Dressing neatly and being prepared for an interview can help you land the job you want. Look up information about the company ahead of time, and be prepared to discuss ways that you have shown that you can do the job. For example, if you're applying to be a receptionist, give examples of how you schedule things in your own life and that you know how to greet and treat people.

somebody who will be able to get the job done, even if the tasks are not well defined. Seventy-four percent of the students said employers want their employees to work well under pressure and meet deadlines. Sixty-nine percent of the student workers said employers want employees to find creative ways to do their jobs better and faster, while 69 percent also said it is important for employees to be able to work well alongside people from different ethnic backgrounds. Sixty-three percent of the participants said employers want employees who are interested in upgrading their skills and education, while 59 percent said employees should be ready to adapt to changes in the workplace. Fifty-seven percent of the students said employers will expect them to put in long hours for the good of the organization, and 55 percent said it is important for workers to become long-term employees, staying with the same company for many years. Fifty-four percent of the teenagers who participated in the study said being able to write well is an important skill, and 54 percent said being able to work with computers is a skill that employers value.

"This study reveals that students view adult jobs as quite demanding," the Youth and Employment report said. "Boys and girls alike believe their future employers will look for those who are able to handle ambiguity, work under pressure, find creative solutions to get their work done better and faster, and work with diverse groups. . . . Young people today are optimistic about their potential as future workers and ask adults to give them a chance rather than make assumptions about them based on stereotypes."

The Difficulty of Finding Part-Time Work

The U.S. Labor Department, as well as many states, regulate the hours teenagers may work. Generally, teenagers who are 16 and older can work an unlimited number of hours, but students who are 15 and younger are barred from working for more than three hours on school days. Younger teens may also not work hours that begin before 7 A.M. or end after 7 P.M. Those laws were established to avoid the abusive child-labor practices common in the 19th century and early years of the 20th century, when young boys were forced to work from before dawn until after dusk in dark and dirty coal mines while young girls were forced to toil for long hours as seamstresses in clothing factories, working for mere pennies.

But there is no getting around the difficulties teenagers face in finding after-school jobs when the economy simply is not healthy enough to provide these kinds of positions. When full-time jobs for adults become hard to find, many older workers take lesser-paying jobs that would ordinarily go to teenagers. The Bureau of Labor Statistics has found that millions of American adults must work at multiple part-time jobs so that they can, in essence, earn the equivalent of a full-time paycheck. This is because full-time jobs have become harder to find since 2007, when the United States endured a period known as an economic recession. A recession occurs when the economy stops growing, and businesses close or cut their workforces, meaning there are fewer jobs.

According to the National Bureau of Economic Research, there have been 10 economic recession periods between 1948 and 2011. The most recent recession began in December 2007; although it is considered to have ended in 2009, by 2013 the U.S. economy had still not fully recovered. The unemployment rate, which had been around 4 to 5 percent before the recession, rose gradually over the next few years, reaching 10 percent in October 2009. Although it has slowly come down, in May 2013 the unemployment rate remained around 7.5 percent, according to the Bureau of Labor Statistics. About 7.6 million Americans who wanted to work more hours were stuck in part-time jobs—a figure that was 65 percent higher than the number before the recession began in 2007.

"There's nothing inherently wrong with people taking part-time jobs if they want them," explained economist Diane Swonk. "The problem is that people are accepting part-time pay because they have no other choice."

Clearly, teenagers seeking part-time employment have been hurt by the 2007-09 recession and the subsequent slow recovery. According to data from the U.S. Census Bureau, in 2012 less than 30 percent of American teens were able to find a summer job. Teens were forced to compete against adults for the same types of part-time jobs that were available to young people in previous years.

Marketable Skills

Not all teenagers stock shelves in convenience stores, work at car washes, or sell jewelry in mall kiosks. Even in the dimmest economic times, some teenagers recognize that they have marketable skills and are savvy enough to put them to work to earn money. Leigh Taylor, who grew up in Oklahoma, works between 10 and 12 hours a week training horses. The 17-year-old student had been riding her own horse in area competitions when she was asked to train another girl's horse. Soon, she was earning about $400 a month in this part-time job. Leigh spends about half the money she earns on clothes and school expenses, while saving the other half for college.

In Hawaii, 13-year-old Alejandra Torres carved herself out a niche as one of the busiest babysitters on the island of Oahu. While growing up in Kentucky she had watched other people's dogs, but she switched to babysitting after her family moved to a mostly pet-free military base near Honolulu. Word soon spread among the military families, and Alejandra became very busy. She works on average approximately 10 hours per week and earns about $120 a month, most of which she saves for college. A true entrepreneur, Alejandra told *USA Today* that she has plans to recruit other teens to set up a babysitters' club to pool jobs.

Chapter Three

A student enters data into a computer under the eye of a doctor at a veterinary hospital. Many schools now offer programs in which students can serve apprenticeships in various career fields.

Career Training in High School

Edward Ortiz hardly resembled a typical 16-year-old as he stood behind a teller's window at a Milwaukee bank. Dressed in a pinstriped shirt and red tie, the student at Riverside University High School spent four afternoons a week at the bank, getting hands-on experience in customer service, marketing, and financial operations. His mornings were spent in class at Riverside High. Edward told a reporter for *Education Week* magazine that after graduation from high school, he intended to enroll at the University of Wisconsin as the next step in what he hoped would be a career in banking. "Now that I know how the banking industry really works, I have a better understanding for it," he said. "I know it's not just going to get a check cashed or to deposit money. It's much more complicated than that."

At 17, Eddie Hwang also dressed quite differently from the normal teenager. He spent part of

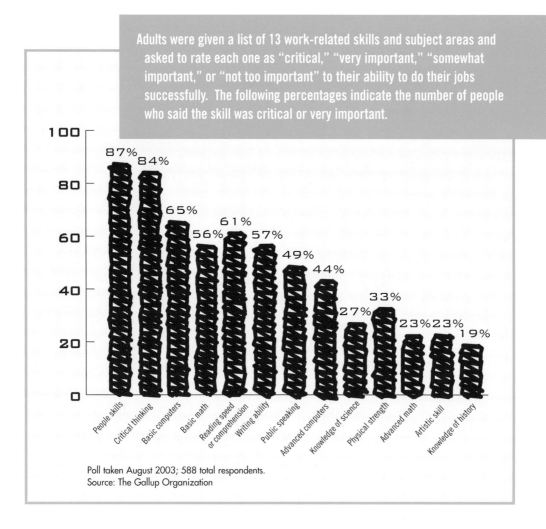

Adults were given a list of 13 work-related skills and subject areas and asked to rate each one as "critical," "very important," "somewhat important," or "not too important" to their ability to do their jobs successfully. The following percentages indicate the number of people who said the skill was critical or very important.

Poll taken August 2003; 588 total respondents.
Source: The Gallup Organization

his school day wearing a lab coat with a stethoscope slung around his neck. The student from Kalamazoo, Michigan, worked part-time at Bronson Methodist Hospital, where he assisted the staff while gaining experience for his future career, which he hoped would be in medicine. "He does everything that we do," cardiovascular technician Jennifer Fleser told *Education Week*. "No special treatment."

In the United States, nearly every high school and even many middle schools provide some type of career counseling or preparation programs. Some schools leave it to guidance counselors to help teenagers take the first tentative steps on their career paths.

Other districts take career planning much further. Some districts, like the ones attended by Edward Ortiz and Eddie Hwang, have established youth apprenticeship programs to enable students to receive hands-on training at job sites. Other districts have started "career academies," which enable students to concentrate on the courses that will help them the most in the careers they have selected. That's what Stacey Connors had to do as a ninth-grade student at New Haven High School in Michigan. Stacey was interested in a medical career, so she was encouraged to take biology, anatomy, and physiology courses. Many career academies also give students the chance to obtain on-the-job training, sometimes with pay.

Job Shadowing

Today, the type of programs that gave Eddie Hwang and Edward Ortiz their first career exposures are more the exception than the rule. The Education Department says there are about 1,500 career academies in operation in U.S. high schools. A similar program is the "High Schools That Work" consortium of more than 1,200 schools in 30 states and the District of Columbia, which follow a plan that includes teaching rigorous academic skills valued by employers.

While those numbers would appear to suggest that career training is available to tens of thousands of students, that is not necessarily the case. In most instances, students who are accepted for youth apprenticeships, career academies, and the High Schools That Work program must go through extensive screening processes designed to accept only the students most committed to career preparation. "It's a lot of studying," Kim Keller admitted to *Education Week*. Keller, a student at Comstock High School in Michigan, had been accepted into a youth apprenticeship program designed for prospective nurses. Her career training started in the 10th grade when, in addition to her high school classes, she also reported for training at Bronson Methodist Hospital. Part of Kim's year was spent "job shadowing" a professional in the health-care field, meaning that Kim and other students tagged along with employees, watching how they carried out their duties.

As high-school juniors, Kim and other youth apprentices spent their afternoons at the hospital or at the local community college taking courses in such areas as nutrition, disease prevention, basic cardiac life support, medical terminology, cell biology, and health-related mathematics. As seniors, the students were encouraged to take more college-level courses. Kim told *Education Week* it did not take her long to realize that there were many differences between the standard high school courses she was taking at Comstock and the career-oriented courses that the hospital was teaching.

Career academies offer even more hands-on training. In most cases, a career academy is established by a high school and made available to a select number of students. The career academy concentrates on a particular course of study; usually, the same teacher stays with the class from start to finish. Lake Clifton-Eastern High School in Maryland has established a career academy devoted to financial studies. Students learn to understand financial publications, take courses in economics, and job-shadow bankers and other financial professionals. They can take courses at Morgan State University or participate in salaried summer internships at Maryland corporations. Lake Clifton-Eastern's career academy is selective—98 percent of its graduates go on to college, while the rest of the Lake Clifton-Eastern student body has a college attendance rate of just 16 percent.

More typical, perhaps, is a career academy devoted to graphic arts established by Pasadena High School in California. A classroom in the high school was set aside for the academy. It is equipped with computers, printing presses, cutting machines, and a photo darkroom, all donated to the school by the Printing Industries Association of Southern California, a trade group that agreed to support the academy. Students enter as sophomores and remain through their senior years. At Pasadena High School, the graphic arts students still take courses offered to other students, but even those

Internships and job shadowing programs can help teenagers get a head start on a future career. A U.S. Department of Education study said, "Career-related education might be a good way of teaching all of the . . . skills valued by employers: academic skills, computer skills, and basic work behaviors."

courses are tailored for career training. For example, in English class the students were given the assignment of writing autobiographical essays. Then, in graphic arts class, they were assigned to convert their essays to print, performing tasks that included page layout and design, desktop publishing, binding, and printing. Along the way, they were required to use mathematics skills to determine the production costs, and then business-writing skills to draft letters explaining the project.

Learning Workplace Etiquette

The Pasadena program and other career academies and youth apprenticeship plans would not succeed without support from the business community, which provides financial assistance, mentors, and other resources. The reason for corporate support is quite obvious: businesses would rather hire young people they have helped to train. By participating in their education, businesses can be assured that teenagers learn workplace etiquette — how to dress for work, how to show up on time, and how to conduct themselves in a professional manner. What's more, though, businesses can help guarantee themselves a source of qualified employees. In Binghamton, New York, for example, Anitec — a manufacturer of film, paper and chemical products for the graphic arts industry — saw its local labor pool drying up. Typically, Anitec liked to hire graduates of two-year technical colleges with strong backgrounds in mathematics and science. Company recruiters looked to the local community college for qualified applicants, but by the early 1990s it became apparent to Anitec that fewer and fewer students in the Binghamton area were graduating from the community college with the training that Anitec desired.

To fill this gap Anitec established its own youth apprenticeship program for Binghamton-area high school students. This gave an opportunity for young people like James Kasmarcik to get great work experiences. James, a student at Susquehanna Valley High School, got a job analyzing the patterns of thousands of tiny dots that compose a printed photograph. He examined the sharpness of the dots through an optical microscope, then used a computer to assess the quality of the photographs that were produced with products manufactured by Anitec. Looking over James's shoulder was an Anitec employee who served as the student's mentor. The program was praised by students and educators; unfortunately, it didn't help save the company, which went out of business in 2011.

Evidence suggests that young people who take part in career preparation programs in their high schools not only do well in the job-related portions of their training, but they excel in academic areas as well. Students who enroll in a High Schools That Work curriculum are subjected to rigorous reading, mathematics, and science courses that are believed to be of practical use to employers. "Students in the general track of most high schools do not meet the typical college entry requirements, nor do they complete an adequate number of credits in a specific career-technical specialty," said the education department study. "Career-bound students in High Schools That Work are expected to meet both of these challenges. The recommended courses in High Schools That Work blend the essential content of college-preparatory mathematics, science and language arts courses with modern career-technical studies in grades 9 through 12."

Enrollment in career academies, youth apprenticeships, and similar programs is often limited, and many students wish such opportunities were available. When students sound off about what is wrong with their schools, they often complain that the classes they take do not prepare them for their future careers. In 1996 and 1997, the Gallup Youth Survey polled 500 young people about how they would grade the quality of teaching in their schools. Just 18 percent said they would give an "A" to the vocational training that was made available to them.

In another Gallup Youth Survey, 517 young people were asked this question: "Thinking now about your high school/middle school, do you have any ideas for changes your school could make to help students learn better? What are they?" Some of the students suggested better career preparation. One 15-year-boy voiced a common complaint. "We need classes that will help us get jobs after high school or we are lost," he said. "We need metal shop classes, automotive, woodshop, etc. We have nothing now. We need these jobs to make a living or help us go to college." And a 16-year-old girl said, "I just think that they should make certain vocational programs, like business and marketing, able to fit in an Advanced Placement student's schedule."

Opportunities for College Students

Students who go to college will find many more opportunities for career preparation awaiting them. For example, many colleges make use of working professionals to teach practical courses, leaving the theory courses in the hands of the professors and other full-time faculty members. It means, for example, that a newspaper editor may be hired to teach a class in journalism or a corporate executive may be retained to lead a class in management or a marketing director may be called in to teach an advertising class. These working professionals provide their students with an insider's view of real on-the-job situations.

Most colleges also regard internships as vital parts of their students' education. Rare is the college that does not give credits to students who obtain internships. Rare, also, is the college that does not maintain an active internship program, staffed by professionals whose duties include the recruitment of businesses to provide slots—both paid and unpaid—to students.

In 2012, a survey by the National Association of Colleges and Employers found that 60 percent of the students who graduated from college that spring and had taken part in a paid internship program received at least one job offer. This was considerably higher than the rate of job offers to graduates who had served unpaid internships (37 percent) or no internship experience (36 percent).

"Experience is frequently cited by employers as to what makes the student an attractive job candidate," says Brent A. Stewart, associate director of career services at The Citadel, a college in South Carolina. "Internships also help students prepare for the transition from school to work."

College students who serve internships can take advantage of many opportunities. In addition to on-the-job training, as well as an inside track toward full-time employment with the company providing the internship, they also get to meet other professionals in the field, who may tell them about job opportunities elsewhere. "Networking" is a common practice in the corporate world, and student interns soon learn how to make best use of the contacts they make.

Most interns appreciate the experience. Jared Kareiner majored in English literature at Marymount Manhattan College in New York City. Jared decided he wanted to work in public relations, so he found an unpaid internship working in the promotions depart-

A representative of the U.S. Secret Service speaks with a group of young women at a career fair in Chicago. Networking helps young job-seekers find employment.

ment of *W Magazine*. Working for free, Jared put in 16 hours a week. When the internship ended, Jared found another internship, this time with a salary, writing press releases for a career counseling firm in New York. Jared barely made enough money to cover his living expenses, but knew he had made the right decision. He told a reporter for the *Boston Globe*, "The friends I had who did not do any internships before they graduated are now doing things like waiting tables. They don't have good jobs. I think most employers are looking for people who can hit the ground running and not just somebody with a degree."

Erin Robinson, a political science student at Brigham Young University, found an internship in Washington, D.C., on the staff of U.S. Senator Harry Reid of Nevada. She told her school's news service, "I chose to intern in D.C. for two reasons. I am a political science major and I felt to really understand politics I needed to be there. I thought it was ridiculous that we had piles of textbooks and were learning it, but didn't get to see it."

Erin's experience in the nation's capital should also help put to rest the notion that college interns are usually assigned mundane, boring duties such as running a copy machine or sorting the mail. In Erin's case, she assisted Senator Reid at congressional hearings and other important events. "I was in the right place at the right time to experience so many things, meet so many people and increase my chances of getting a better job," said Erin.

Erin Robinson and Jared Kareiner may not have been typical college students, however. Both of those young people seemed to have a good idea of what they wanted to do when they got to college and how to achieve their career goals. The fact that many U.S. college students do not declare a major until after their freshman or sophomore years suggests that many teenagers do not know where their career paths may be heading.

Chapter Four

For many young people who go to college, selecting a major is a difficult task. Students may have a hard time determining a career path when they are still learning who they are and what they want to accomplish in their lives.

Picking a Career in College

Dave Sheeran was preparing for his freshman year at the University of Cincinnati. When a newspaper reporter asked the 18-year-old student from Loveland, Ohio, what he planned to declare as a major, Dave answered, "I have no clue. I'm planning on going my first two years undecided, and I'm hoping I'll have a good idea after that."

Another freshman who entered college without declaring a major was Jacquie Illig, who was one of 239 undeclared members of the freshman class at Fairfield University in Connecticut that year. "I'm undeclared because I don't want to make a decision too quickly," Jacquie told her school newspaper. "I want to get acquainted with all the different subjects first and the core allows me to do that."

For more than 8 million students a year, the path toward a career starts with college. Like Dave and Jacquie, many students are unsure of where their lives are headed. In 2002, the Los Angeles-based

Higher Education Research Institute reported that 8.4 percent of that year's college freshmen did not declare a major. In 1966, the institute reported, just 1.7 percent of freshmen had been undeclared. Betsy Barefoot, co-director of the North Carolina-based Policy Center on the First Year of College, told the *Cincinnati Enquirer*, "It's unrealistic to think all 18-year-olds can decide what they want to do, but colleges and universities are taking greater responsibility in helping students make those decisions."

Many schools have now assigned counselors to work with undeclared students who are having trouble picking majors. Many schools also run career fairs and invite professionals to speak with the students about what their jobs are all about. At Arkansas State University, for example, the school started requiring all undeclared students to begin meeting with faculty advisors. In just one year, the school saw the number of undeclared students drop by half. The school started the policy because it had been seeing too many of its students reach their junior and senior years without declaring a major.

Students who do not declare a major typically take a variety of liberal arts or general studies courses. They may take classes in English, history, political science, sociology, psychology, mathematics, and the sciences. While those classes are important—and to some degree required of many students regardless of their major—students with declared majors soon find their schedules dominated by courses that will help train them for the careers they have selected. Meanwhile, the general studies student drifts from class to class. When this student finally declares a major, he or she may have to double-up on required classes in order to graduate on time. If the student has waited too long, he or she may find himself enrolling for a fifth year in a college program that was supposed to take only four years to complete. In fact, the American College on Education has found that the average time it takes to complete a bachelor's degree is now 5.5 years.

Students may simply be stunned by the number of choices available to them. At big colleges like the California State University campus in Fullerton, which has an enrollment of more than 31,000 undergraduates, students can select from more than 200 majors. Is it any wonder that in a typical semester some 1,400 incoming Cal State Fullerton freshmen will be undeclared? "Sometimes, students are just overwhelmed by the number of majors that we have," Carol May, a Fullerton academic advisor, told a reporter for her school's student newspaper. "They may have many different interests and don't know how to narrow down their options."

Just as troubling to college administrators is the student who decides after a few years that he or she has picked the wrong major. This unfortunate student has to virtually start over with a new major. At Cal State Fullerton, administrators work with incoming freshmen to make sure they understand their major and its requirements and are aware of what types of jobs await them when they graduate. Fullerton freshman programs coordinator Jennifer Lukridge told her school's newspaper that it is not unusual for as much as 85 percent of a college's student body to change majors at least once.

Students at smaller colleges don't often run into the dilemma of having too many options for a major. At some small schools, it is not unusual to find just a handful of majors available to students. But if a student decides he or she has picked the wrong major, there may not be many other choices available at the school. This could mean the student must either settle for an undesirable career field or transfer to another college in order to find a suitable major. College officials hope that with the right counseling, students can avoid such errors.

Why Go to College?

College represents different opportunities to different students. There is the opportunity to live away from home for the first time. There is the opportunity to meet new friends. There are the football games, fraternity parties, and other social events. There is no question, though, that virtually all students enroll in college to prepare for their careers. That is what 95 percent of all incoming freshmen told researchers for the University of North Carolina who conducted a study on student attitudes at the Asheville campus in 2000. Other reasons cited in the study were participation in college social life; development of critical thinking; learning more about science, the arts and the humanities, and a desire to live away from home.

Young people understand the importance of a college education, according to the Gallup Youth Survey. A 1999 survey of 502 young people between the ages of 13 and 17 reported that even the children of parents who did not attend college knew the importance of college. When both parents had attended college, 99 percent of the respondents said that a college education is either "very important" or "somewhat important." When neither of a

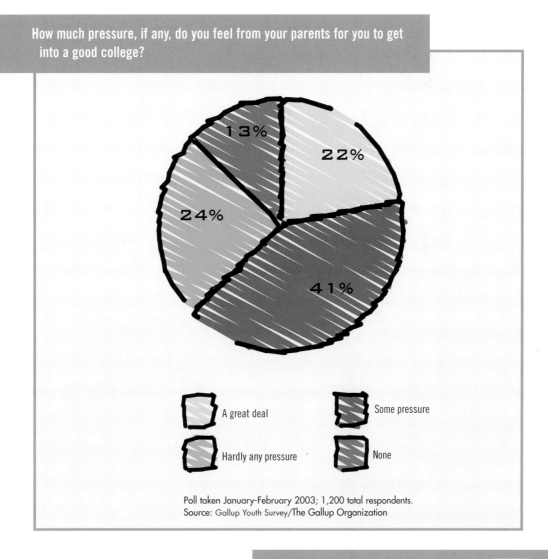

How much pressure, if any, do you feel from your parents for you to get into a good college?

13%

22%

24%

41%

A great deal

Some pressure

Hardly any pressure

None

Poll taken January-February 2003; 1,200 total respondents.
Source: Gallup Youth Survey/The Gallup Organization

student's parents had attended the college, the response was not much lower. In that case, 98 percent of the respondents said a college education is "very important" or "somewhat important."

In 1979, the Gallup Youth Survey reported that many teens said they would be satisfied if, after high school, they attained secure, high-paying employment in blue-collar jobs. When asked, for example, whether they would want a blue-collar job that paid $30,000 a year or a white-collar job that would pay $20,000 a year, 66 percent of the respondents opted for the blue-collar job. However, the Gallup Organization's researchers found that the students who aspired for white-collar jobs knew that they would find greater economic success as their careers progressed.

Young people's attitudes changed greatly over the next two decades. In polls taken in 2000 and 2001, the Gallup Youth Survey found that teens were more interested in careers that require college, such as medicine, the law, and computer science. In 2001, the Gallup Youth Survey asked 501 teens about their plans after high school, and 63 percent reported that they intended to enroll in college as full-time students. A similar poll taken in 1983 reported that just 46 percent of teenagers planned to enroll as full-time students following their college graduations.

There is no secret about this shift: college graduates simply earn more money than people who have not graduated from college. According to the Bureau of Labor Statistics, the median salary for a college graduate in 2012 was $55,432, while the median salary for somebody with just a high school diploma was $33,904. In other words, college graduates can expect to earn salaries that are nearly twice as high as people without degrees. (High school students thinking about dropping out should reconsider: the Bureau of Labor Statistics reports that someone without a high school diploma can expect to earn a median salary of just $24,492 a year—44 percent of what a college graduate earns.)

The Bureau of Labor Statistics believes that there should be many opportunities awaiting employees who are just entering the job market by 2020. If those employees have college degrees, the government agency says, the outlook could not be better. Because of the expected retirements of college-educated baby-boomers, the number of job openings for college-educated individuals will roughly equal the number of recent college graduates looking for work.

Popular Majors

Not all college students register as undeclared majors. If 8 percent of students are undecided, 92 percent of students have declared a

Although 95 percent of freshmen say they enrolled in college to prepare for their career, meeting people of other backgrounds and participating in campus activities are also important aspects of the college experience.

Graduation from college is worth celebrating—studies show that the average college graduate can expect to earn more than twice as much as the average worker with only a high-school diploma.

major and are actively working toward degrees in their fields of choice. According to the Princeton Review, a publisher of college admissions test preparatory manuals, the 10 most popular majors on college campuses in 2012 were, in the following order: business administration or management; psychology; nursing; biology; education; English language and literature; economics; communications; political science; and computer or information science.

Many of those majors have been popular for years, but college administrators report that other majors have gained in popularity over the past few years. In many cases, majors become more popular because of changing trends in society, events in the news, or because a particular profession has become intriguing to young people through its portrayal in popular culture. At Baylor University in Texas, for example, so many students entered the school's forensic science major that college officials were forced to establish a minimum grade-point average in the program and cap the number of students permitted to enroll. Forensic scientists help solve crimes by performing the chemical and biological analyses at crime scenes. The University of West Virginia saw enrollment in its forensic science program double within one year. College officials believe the popularity of such crime-related TV shows as *CSI: Crime Scene Investigation*, which dramatizes forensic investigations, has led to the increases in enrollment.

Other majors gaining in popularity in recent years are health-related programs, social studies, international studies, courses dealing with aviation, and religious studies. College administrators believe American involvement in conflicts in the Middle East may have helped boost interest in religious studies, particularly Islam.

Ironically, the corporate scandals that were very much in the news a few years ago led to a heightened interest in business-related programs, particularly accounting. Accountants keep track of how much money comes into a business and how much money goes out. At some large companies, such as Texas-based Enron, accountants were accused of reporting phony numbers so that the value of the company's stock would rise, making high-ranking corporate executives wealthy. It would seem that such negative publicity might turn young people off to the idea of becoming accountants, but administrators at Arizona State

University found the opposite to be true. Rather than drive young people away from accounting as a career, college administrators found that the publicity made students aware of what the profession is all about. And certainly, as students, the future

STRENGTHSQUEST

Career counselors generally urge young people to find career fields that have a strong interest for them, or that they are temperamentally suited for. The StrengthsQuest program developed by the Gallup Organization is a unique way for students to learn about their strengths and how to best use them for academic and career success.

"Our intention was to give students an understanding of their strengths, how they can use these strengths to help them have better success in school, and how to make better career choices," explained StrengthsQuest consultant Irene Burklund. "We want to give students ideas to think about while looking into careers, rather than telling them what careers they should choose."

The StrengthsQuest program consists of three primary components. Students begin by taking the StrengthsFinder assessment—180 questions intended to provide them information about their greatest areas of talent. Once the assessment is completed, a personalized web page is created for the student, which will focus on the five areas identified as the student's greatest strengths. Students also receive a 320-page book called *StrengthsQuest: Discover your Strengths in Academics, Career, and Beyond*, which provides study techniques and methods for academic planning, based on their strengths, that can help them to succeed in college or in finding the career that is right for them. The StrengthsQuest book and web site help students develop their talents into strengths and apply those strengths to completing school and choosing the right career.

More information about the StrengthsQuest program is available at www.strengthsquest.com.

accountants would hopefully learn ethics and a sense of responsibility.

Computer careers remain among the fastest-growing fields in society. In 2013 William Kamela, the senior policy counsel for Microsoft, spoke about the need for people trained in computer science and engineering. He said that the United States produces 40,000 computer science graduates each year, but that companies like Microsoft, Intel, and other American firms need more than 120,000 a year. The average annual salary for such jobs is well over $100,000, Kamela said.

All students who graduate from college finish their education with a degree in something. Most college students seem pretty happy with the majors they select. Typical, perhaps, is Fairfield student Erin Joyce, who started her college career as an accounting major but quickly decided she had made a mistake. Erin told her school newspaper, "I was not enjoying my major classes as much as my friends were so I decided to change to marketing, a subject that excited me a lot more than accounting. I think a lot of people go into accounting because it is the easiest to get a job in afterwards; however, I think enjoying your work is much more important."

Chapter Five

Vo-tech schools attract some of the most motivated students and train them in such trades as construction, cosmetology, and cooking. However, studies show that fewer students are interested in careers in the trades today.

Tackling
the Trades

Plenty of students go to school. How many of them help build a school building? That's what about 40 vocational students in Springfield, Ohio, helped to do. For nearly a year, the students at Springfield-Clark Joint Vocational School gave up their study halls, lunch periods, and often their Saturdays to help erect their school's new administration building. Carpentry students framed the building, plumbing students ran the pipe work, and student electricians connected the wiring. In all, the Springfield-Clark students performed about 90 percent of the work on the building, saving their school district's taxpayers about $200,000 in labor costs. "We're young, but that makes no difference," Springfield-Clark student Alan Keefer told a reporter for the Associated Press. "We have a job to do and we're expected to do it well and learn new things as we go."

In McKinney, Texas, cosmetology students spend three hours every morning in "cosmetology lab," where they don smocks and practice clipping and setting hair. Some of the girls in the class at McKinney High School enrolled simply for a diversion from their regular studies, but some girls do have intentions of becoming professional hair stylists. April Crain, for example, told a reporter for the *McKinney Messenger* that most of the women in her family worked as hair stylists, and she expected to carry on the family tradition following graduation. "My grandmother did it, my two aunts," she said. "I grew up watching them do hair."

Not everybody goes to a four-year college. There are many careers available in the trades, where skilled workers continue to be in demand. Computers may have changed the way of life for most Americans, but it still takes a skilled pair of hands to rebuild a carburetor. The health-care field may be the fastest growing area of employment in the United States, but doctors and nurses can't work in a hospital unless there are carpenters, masons, ironworkers, and other tradesmen to build it.

The number of young people who don't attend or finish a four-year college program is higher than the number who do. According to the U.S. Education Department, some two-thirds of young people do not obtain a bachelor's degree, and about 25 percent of all teenagers go right to full-time work after high school. Where do they find work? For many of them, their career paths take them to the trades. "The reality is that most young people must draw on skills learned outside of four-year colleges to succeed in the workforce," said a report on vocational education compiled by the U.S. Education Department. "That's where good career and technical education at secondary schools and communityand technical colleges comes in."

College-educated individuals generally earn higher salaries than people who don't go to college. That does not necessarily mean that young people without college degrees have to settle for low-paying jobs, however. According to the most recent Bureau of Labor Statistics, typical salaries for experienced trades workers include carpenters, $39,530; brick masons, $45,410; drywall installers, $38,290; electricians, $48,250; painters, $34,280; plumbers, $46,600; roofers, $34,220; cosmetologists, $22,500; and chefs, $40,630. The holders of those jobs can expect to settle into comfortable, middle-class lifestyles.

Still, the number of high school students electing to study the trades has remained stagnant for a number of years. "For the most part, there has been little change in who participates in vocational education over the last decade," the Education Department report said. "Vocational education serves a diverse set of students, with

Careers in the culinary arts have long been popular among teenage boys.

Gallup Youth Survey results suggest that boys and girls between the ages of 13 and 17 view the importance of a college education differently. Girls are more likely to plan to go to college full time than are boys, and that gap has widened over time. The chart below shows the percentage of girls and boys who say they would like to attend college full time after leaving high school, as tracked by the Gallup Youth Survey over two decades.

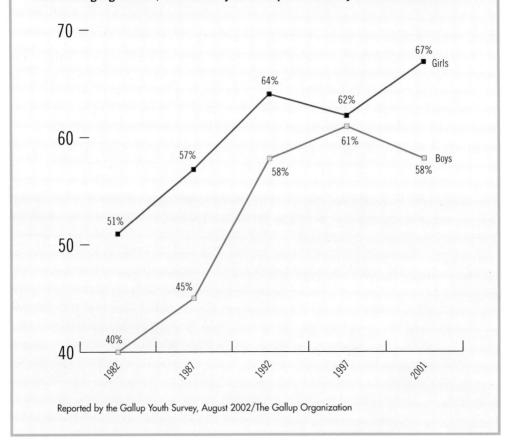

Reported by the Gallup Youth Survey, August 2002/The Gallup Organization

most coming from the middle range of academic and income advantage. . . . some groups continue to participate more substantially than others: students who enter high school with low academic achievement, have disabilities, are male, English-language proficient, or from lower-income or rural schools. Gender differences remain. Girls' vocational course taking has been declining while that of boys has remained consistent."

Academic Achievement

There are several reasons for the lack of growth in vocational education. For starters, high schools have placed more emphasis on academic achievement, shifting resources into college-preparatory courses. On the one hand, that has meant less money for vocational training. On the other hand, though, it has meant that more and more students heading for the trades are exposed to college-level academics. Educators believe this is not necessarily a bad policy, given the fact that many vocational students do attend community or technical colleges, and many employers are looking for employees who can work with their heads as well as their hands. Patricia W. McNeil, an assistant secretary in the U.S. Education Department, told *Education Week*, "The old 'voc-ed' designed for the industrial age is not going to work anymore. We need to help people understand the needs of the workplace have changed."

Educators and government officials know how important vocational training is to the 11 million high school, community college, and private vocational school students who are preparing for jobs in the trades. Under the Carl D. Perkins Vocational and Technical Education Act, the U.S. government makes available some $1.3 billion a year to high school vo-tech programs. There are currently about 11,000 high schools in America that provide training in the trades, including 1,400 schools dedicated solely to vo-tech training, usually supported by several school districts in a single region or county. Also, vocational training has not been left out of the youth apprenticeship, career academy, and High Schools That Work programs.

Vocational students enrolled in such programs say they are grateful to receive hands-on training from true professionals. For example, printing apprentice Schenita Henderson, 17, of Milwaukee, told a reporter for *Education Week* that her apprenticeship called for her to spend mornings at Milwaukee Trade and Technical High School followed by afternoons on the job at a local printing company. "You learn a faster way of doing things and a more precise way," Schenita said. "Other students who aren't in the program, they have to wait to find out what it might be like to work in a company. But I have the experience now, and I know what positions are available."

Vocational students are serious about their futures. A study performed by educators in New York State found that within 18 months of graduation, 91 percent of vo-tech students were either working in the trades, had joined the military, or had enrolled in college.

Vo-tech teachers often tell stories of how students suddenly blossom in their classrooms as they learn how to use tools and discover skills they never knew they possessed. In Locust Creek, North Carolina, for example, Arlin Middleton, vocational director for the school system of Jackson County, beamed as he watched students from Smoky Mountain High School erect a home that served as a project for the vocational classes. While it would have taken a private contractor just a few months to build the home, the Smoky Mountain students took three years to do the work, mostly because of the limitations put on class time. Still, Middleton was pleased with what he saw: carpentry students framing the house, electrical students wiring the house, plumbing students installing the bathroom fixtures, and woodworking students building the custom kitchen cabinets. Middleton pointed out that some of the students who started work on the project had already graduated and were working full time in the trades by the time the finishing touches were put on the dwelling, which the school district intended to sell so that future vo-tech projects could be financed. "It is an exceptionally well-built house," Middleton told a reporter for the local newspaper. "Our students have done a great job."

Despite such success stories, the Gallup Youth Survey confirms a dwindling interest from young people in vocational education and, therefore, in careers in the trades. In 1979, a poll of 1,115 young people between the ages of 13 and 17 concluded that the top career choices among boys were jobs in the trades, such as mechanic and electrician. The top career choice for girls that year was secretary.

In 1995, the Gallup Youth Survey again asked the question of 518 teenagers, and this time trades-related jobs ranked no higher than 10th among boys. As for girls, the highest ranking trades-related job was cosmetologist, which ranked eighth. A career choice of secretary has not made the list since 1988, when it ranked eighth. And a 2003 survey on teens' top career choices found the careers of mechanic and chef on the list, but well below the most popular choices.

What has all this meant for young people who do decide to become skilled carpenters, mechanics, chefs, and cosmetologists? According to the U.S. Education Department, it means there will be plenty of jobs waiting for them. Perhaps they will need a bit more training than they can get in high school, which they can probably find at a community or technical college or private vocational school.

Young people learning the carpentry, plumbing, and electrical trades have an opportunity to practice their skills with such organizations as Habitat for Humanity. In addition, some vo-tech schools purchase houses in need of repair, let the students gain experience by doing the work, and then sell the properties to fund future projects.

Proud of Their Talents

Students heading for jobs in the trades say they are satisfied with their career choices and proud of their talents. In Falmouth, Virginia, vo-tech students spent most of 2003 building a house as a class project. The three-bedroom ranch home featured a two-car garage, country kitchen, deck, two-and-a-half baths, and walk-in closets, and was to be sold by the school district for a price estimated at $240,000, with the profit plowed into the next year's vocational project. Stafford High School students Jason Johncox and Josh Pitts both worked on the house. "Nobody at our school even knows about this," said a proud Jason as he showed off the house to a newspaper reporter. "Yeah," added Josh. "All we had in the yearbook was a group picture."

Vo-tech classes at Fairfield High School in California also perform building projects. In some cases, students are assigned to the local chapter of Habitat for Humanity, which rehabilitates old houses, then makes them available for low-income first-time home buyers. One of the student carpenters, 18-year-old Carlos Romero, told a reporter for the Fairfield *Daily Republic* that thanks to his experience he is able to find part-time construction work on weekends earning $15 an hour.

In San Antonio, Texas, woodworking students entered a competition to design and build playhouses and sheds. Taft High School student Daniel Zamarripa used his skills to design and build a playhouse that resembled a sailing ship, which he nicknamed the U.S.S. *Raider*. The 16-year-old told the *San Antonio Express-News*, "I wanted to make something that was hard, not just another shed."

And in Arizona, Ana Peña, a 17-year-old senior at Metro Tech High School in Phoenix, was among more than 130 vo-tech students who competed at a statewide construction skills competition. Ana told a reporter for the *Arizona Republic* that she chose carpentry as a career path because of the job prospects that awaited her after high school. She said, "I can graduate from high school and earn $30,000 or more a year as a carpenter. That's what got me hooked."

Chapter Six

Soldiers climb over obstacles during their basic training at Fort Benning, Georgia. The military is an attractive option to many high-school graduates because it offers training in a variety of careers to soldiers on active duty, and provides money for higher education after they leave the service.

Basic Training and Beyond

In early 2004, as U.S. soldiers faced hostilities in Iraq, Afghanistan, and elsewhere, three teenage girls in Merced County, California, walked into the local army recruiting office to enlist. One of the girls, Rachel Leon, told a reporter for the *Merced Sun-Star* that she was aware American soldiers were facing danger in combat; nevertheless, she aimed for a career in law enforcement and believed the U.S. Army would provide the fastest route toward her goal. Rachel hoped to join the ranks of the military police. "I decided if I go to college, I have to wait four or five years until I start working and doing what I wanted," Rachel told the newspaper. "And, I just wanted to do it quicker. I don't want to sit down and wait forever and when I'm 30, start to do my job. I want to start my future now. So, I decided to join the Army."

The other two girls were also looking forward to joining the U.S. Army. Both Shelly Ambron and Liliana Hurtado had been planning to enlist in the

WHICH BRANCH OF THE ARMED FORCES IS MOST IMPORTANT TO OUR NATIONAL DEFENSE TODAY?

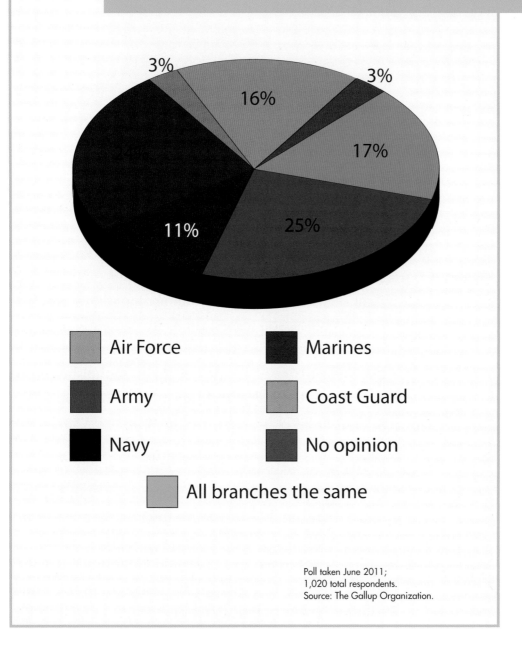

3%
16%
3%
24%
17%
11%
25%

Air Force

Army

Navy

Marines

Coast Guard

No opinion

All branches the same

Poll taken June 2011;
1,020 total respondents.
Source: The Gallup Organization.

armed services for several years. Both of the 18-year-olds said they knew they could be getting themselves into dangerous situations. Still, to the two teenagers the benefits of military service seemed too good to pass up. Shelly said she hoped to travel across the world and visit places she would never have the opportunity to see if she remained home in California. Liliana told the newspaper that although she recognized the dangers of a career in the military, "I feel like there is something calling me to [serve]. It's something that if I don't do it, I know I'll regret it."

In 2002, as American soldiers fought a war in Afghanistan and prepared for war in Iraq, the four branches of the armed services—army, navy, air force, and marines—met their recruiting goals. A decade later, in 2012, despite the American military being involved in conflicts and peacekeeping missions around the world, the four services again met their recruiting goals. Clearly, stories about violence against U.S. soldiers did not deter young people from choosing the armed services as the next step on their career paths.

Were these young warriors motivated entirely by a sense of patriotism? In the wake of the terrorist attacks of September 2001, perhaps some young people harbored an intense desire to fight for their country. It is more likely, though, that many young people nearing an end to their high school years looked at the career opportunities available in the military and, like Shelly, Liliana, and Rachel, decided to take advantage of them.

Money for College

The four branches of the service have been marketing their career opportunities to young people for years. Television commercials showing young soldiers and sailors receiving training in electronics, aviation technology, engineering, and the sciences are standard fare. In 2001, the U.S. Defense Department published a 367-page book titled simply *Military Careers* and distributed it to libraries throughout the United States. The book contained information on 81 occupations for enlisted personnel and 59 occupations available for officers. The book outlined

MILITARY SERVICE ACADEMIES

In 2003, the Princeton Review released a list of the 10 toughest colleges to get into, based on surveys filled out by more than 100,000 college students. Among the top five were three Ivy League schools—Princeton, Harvard, and Yale. The other two schools making the top five were service academies—the U.S. Military Academy at West Point, New York, and the U.S. Naval Academy in Annapolis, Maryland. West Point beat out the three Ivy League schools, placing first on the Princeton Review's list. West Point trains future army officers while the Naval Academy trains future officers in the navy and marines.

A third service academy, the U.S. Air Force Academy in Colorado Springs also has rigorous standards for admission. Only a handful of students are considered to have the talent and intelligence to enroll in the service academies. To gain entry, students must first be nominated by a member of Congress—either a senator from their state or their representative in the House of Representatives. Typically, most members of Congress appoint review boards that interview the students and recommend a candidate based on their impressions of the student as well as his or her academic, athletic, leadership, and community service records.

Students who are nominated still have to convince the academy to accept them. Academic records, Scholastic Aptitude Test (SAT) scores, and other accomplishments are all taken into account. Admissions officials for the service academies say there are no minimum grade-point averages or SAT scores needed for consideration; nevertheless, competition for places in the academies is fierce. In numerous jobs under the category of "combat specialty occupations" and included the types of jobs one would expect to find in the military, such as artillery and missile crew member, infantry soldier, and special forces commando. But a high school senior browsing through the book would also find that if he joined the armed forces, he could be trained as a court stenographer, plumber, meteorologist, draftsman, cardiopulmonary technician, physical therapist, machinist, printer, welder, TV camera operator,

2012, for example, about 13,000 students sought admission to West Point, and about 4,500 of them received congressional nominations. Only about 1,200 applicants—9 percent of the total applicants—were accepted as students. About three-quarters of the accepted students ranked in the top 20 percent of their classes. Most of the successful applicants had a GPA of 3.5 or higher, and they also tended to have SAT scores above 1800 and an ACT composite score of 25 or higher.

A record of leadership is highly prized by the academies. After all, the schools train students to be officers who could potentially be called on to lead troops into combat. Service academy graduates often remain leaders even after their military careers end. U.S. Presidents Ulysses S. Grant and Dwight D. Eisenhower graduated from West Point, for example, while President Jimmy Carter graduated from the Naval Academy.

"West Point is unique in many ways: a military institution, a first-class university, and a national landmark all rolled into one," a West Point cadet told the authors of the Princeton Review study. "Our motto is 'duty, honor, country,' and sometimes duty looms much larger than the rest. Life is hard here, but its difficulty makes it fulfilling."

foreign language interpreter, photographer, firefighter, air traffic controller, aircraft mechanic, and even musician.

In addition to job training provided by the military, members of the service are also eligible for up to $19,000 for college under a law known as the Montgomery GI Bill. Each branch of the service also maintains college funds, making up to $50,000 available for a soldier's educational needs. And new inductees are often entitled to cash bonuses for as much as $12,000 if they sign on for active duty. In return, new recruits have to serve enlistments that range between two and six years, depending on the program they join. Some young people take advantage of the "delayed entry program," which enables them to enlist in the armed forces but delay the start of their training for up to a year.

When new soldiers do report for duty, their work begins with basic training—a demanding, daily test of physical and mental endurance that typically lasts eight or nine weeks, depending on the service. Next comes advanced training, where the young soldier, sailor, marine, or airman starts learning about the job they signed up for.

The First Job Is to Fight

In the military, young people may be trained as professional emergency medical technicians, communications equipment operators, civil engineers, and nurses. The skills they learn in those occupations can be put to use in the civilian world should they choose to leave the service at the conclusion of their enlistments. In times of war, though, most military-related occupations are put to use in the battlefield. Emergency medical technicians and nurses may have to tend the wounded under fire. Communications equipment operators may have to accompany an infantry brigade into the field to help the combat soldiers stay in contact with their base. Civil engineers and electricians may have to build an airstrip in enemy territory so U.S. planes can land. Although the military offers many jobs, the first job is to fight.

The willingness of young people to fight has declined in recent years. In 1994—three years after the U.S. had quickly won the Gulf War and forced Iraq to withdraw from Kuwait, suffering few casualties in the process—the Gallup Youth Survey queried teenagers on their interest in military careers. In a poll conducted among 508

A recruiter speaks with a young man about the opportunities in the U.S. Army. According to the Gallup Organization, about 38 percent of young people express an interest in serving in the military.

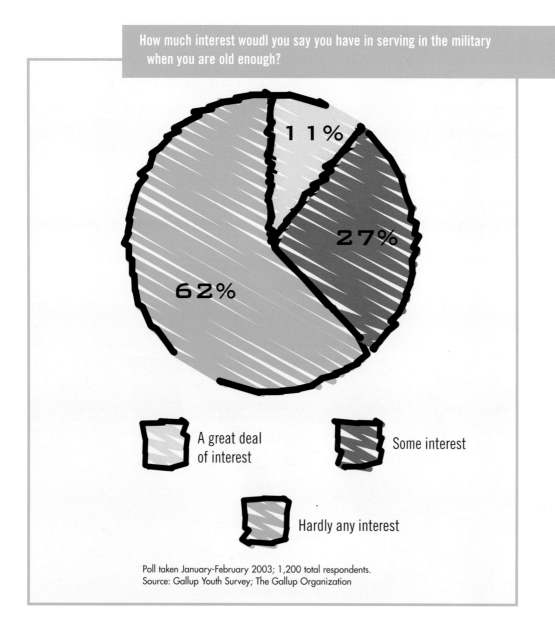

How much interest woudl you say you have in serving in the military when you are old enough?

11%

27%

62%

A great deal of interest

Some interest

Hardly any interest

Poll taken January-February 2003; 1,200 total respondents.
Source: Gallup Youth Survey; The Gallup Organization

teens between the ages of 13 and 17, just 9 percent said they had a "great deal" of interest in a military career, while 13 percent said they had "quite a bit" and 31 percent said they had "some" interest in enlisting. Those numbers indicate that 53 percent of the respondents were willing to give at least some thought toward taking a career path through the military.

Nearly a decade later, as the United States was gearing up for another war against Iraq, young people showed less enthusiasm about military service. In a poll taken in early 2003, on the eve of renewed hostilities against Iraq, just 11 percent of 1,200 young people surveyed had a "great deal" or "quite a bit" of interest in military service, while 27 percent of the respondents said they had "some," for a total of 38 percent willing to consider the military as part of their career path.

This soldier is wearing special gear to protect himself from biological or chemical weapons during a training exercise. The military offers training in hundreds of fields that young people could use once their enlistment is up; however, the first duty of all soldiers is to be ready for combat if necessary.

Despite the war, the four branches of the service each met their recruiting goals in 2003. The goal for the army included recruitment of nearly 74,000 soldiers, while the navy met its goal by signing up more than 41,000 sailors. More than 32,500 young people joined the Marine Corps that year, while more than 37,000 people enlisted in the U.S. Air Force.

The career paths made available by the armed forces motivated many enlistees. Katrese Clayton told *USA Today* that she joined the army after spending a year at Farleigh Dickinson University in New Jersey. "I wasn't thinking about any war," she said. "I was thinking I need help. I was struggling." At the conclusion of her enlistment, Katrese said she hoped to use the army's tuition benefits to return to college and eventually go to law school.

In an essay for *Next Step* magazine, Cornell University Law School graduate Sean-Michael Green said that if it hadn't been for the military, he never would have carved out a successful career. "I graduated from a public high school at the bottom of my class," he wrote. "College was not a practical option for me. Joining the Marine Corps, however, was an option, so I enlisted while I was a high school senior. When I left active duty four years later, I had acquired many experiences that most people my age did not, and I had proven my ability to work through challenges."

Excited About Joining

Of course, some teenagers are drawn to the military because they want to become fighters. That is the career they seek. There is no question the military does emphasize that aspect of the job. The "Army of One" advertising campaign by the U.S. Army typically shows a young soldier using his talents and training to prepare for a dangerous mission. In 2002, the army unveiled a video game titled *America's Army* and made it free on-line for downloading. Within the first year of its release, more than 6 million copies of *America's Army* had been downloaded, and recruiters distributed an additional 2.7 million free copies on CD-Rom to potential recruits. The game was clearly developed with a teenage audience in mind. *America's Army* provides a virtual experience of basic training at Fort Benning, Georgia, complete with a run through an obstacle course and a practice session on the target range. After basic training, players take part in team-oriented missions, which they can play on-line against other virtual soldiers. In one scenario, for example, team members are given the job of defending the Alaska oil pipeline.

Those type of recruiting techniques have helped the armed forces meet their recruiting goals even during a time of war. At a career fair Kenneth Sessoms, a 19-year-old freshman at the New York City College of Technology, found himself drawn to a table set up by an Army recruiter. "I always wanted to join the military," Sessoms told a reporter for *USA Today*. And Stewart County High School senior Ryan Davis, 18, told a reporter for the *Kentucky New Era* that he intended to enlist in the army with the intentions of joining the paratroopers. "Every man in my family has been in the military—my father, my grandfather, my great-grandfather," he said. "I'm excited about joining."

Chapter Seven

Today, greater numbers of young women are interested in careers in scientific or technical fields, breaking the old stereotype that these fields were only for men.

Shattering the Glass Ceiling

Emily Lucks of Naperville, Illinois, was used to working hard: at her high school she was enrolled in an advanced placement physics class and was also involved in three school sports. Nevertheless, after spending a day at Argonne National Laboratory in Illinois, Emily said she would have to prepare herself to work even harder to achieve her dream of a career in science. During her tour, sponsored by the laboratory as part of the "Science Careers in Search of Women" program, Emily and some 230 other teenage girls heard stories from scientists who talked about working late nights, missing summer vacations to study, and taking time off from their careers to raise children. The teenage girls who took part in the program at Argonne spent the day learning about careers in science, listening to panel discussions led by female scientists, and sitting in small groups, where they could discuss their ideas and trepidations about pursuing a career in science. "It didn't really open

Women have come a long way since Oberlin College, the first college for women in the United States, opened in 1833. In 1900, women made up just 19 percent of U.S. college students; today, that figure is over 50 percent.

my eyes, but it just kind of showed me that there are people out there doing this," Emily said after touring the laboratory. "Sometimes I feel like I'm never going to be able to do it, and this conference showed me there are positives to this, that I'm doing everything for a purpose."

Another member of the tour, Tara Weinstein, a 17-year-old student from Buffalo Grove, Illinois, said, "It just makes you really think. I never realized how difficult it was."

A science career "seems so incredibly hectic. I thought it would be easy, but now I know different."

For many young women in the past, the only career in science they could hope to find would be as a nurse in a hospital.

Typically, jobs as doctors, chemists, biologists, and pharmacists went to men. And science was not the only career path that was often closed to women. In the past men dominated most of the management jobs in large corporations, for example.

Times are changing, however. For many women, the road toward equal employment opportunities began in 1963 with adoption of the U.S. Equal Pay Act, which outlawed salary discrimination based on gender. It meant that a company could not maintain a separate wage scale for female and male employees who were performing the same jobs. At the time the law was enacted by Congress, studies showed that women earned an average of 59 cents for every dollar earned by men.

The wage gap has closed some since then, but not entirely. According to the National Partnership For Women And Families, in 2013 women earned 77 cents for each dollar earned by men. Generally, the reason for the disparity is not an unlawful disregard for the law by employers. Instead, the reason for the continuing wage disparity is that men still hold most of the higher-paying jobs.

Women's rights organizations have long charged that a "glass ceiling" exists in corporate America, meaning that women in entry level jobs or middle management positions can look up and see top leadership positions ahead of them, but they cannot break through the invisible barriers of a male-dominated business environment to achieve their goals. The Gallup Youth Survey has found that 76 percent of teenagers believe a glass ceiling does exist for women.

Another reason for the pay disparity is the decision many women make to take time off from their careers to raise children. Many women drop out of the workforce for a dozen years or more, and when they return they find themselves taking jobs that pay less than what men their age are earning, mostly because those men have remained on the job and have been promoted to higher–paying positions. For example, a study by economists at Harvard University concluded that women physicians who are unmarried and have no children earn 13 percent more a year than women physicians who are married, and 15 percent more than women physicians who are raising children. Statistics show that the pay disparity is dramatically reduced among younger workers. Women under the age of 25 earn about 92 cents for every dollar earned by men of the same age. This

TAKING OUR DAUGHTERS AND SONS TO WORK

Each year on the fourth Thursday in April, millions of children take the day off from school to accompany their mothers and fathers to work. "Take Our Daughters and Sons to Work Day" has become an unofficial national holiday, covered by the media and regarded as a significant part of career training for young people.

The event started in 1993 as "Take Our Daughters to Work Day." It was conceived by the Ms. Foundation for Women, an organization established by *Ms.* magazine to encourage girls to envision themselves as productive, career-oriented women. In 2003, it was expanded to include children of both genders.

It is estimated that 44 percent of the parents who take their children to work are fathers. In Kansas City, one of those fathers is Frank Masterson Jr., a manager for Hallmark Cards who brought his daughter Maggie to work. "I want Maggie to go wherever she wants to go, to be appropriately paid and recognized," Masterson told a reporter for the *Christian Science Monitor*. And in Redmond, Washington, Microsoft engineer David Potter brought his daughters Rebecca and Bethany to work with him during the event. He said in a company news release, "I want to expose my kids to both age group includes many young women who have not yet reached the point in their lives when they are thinking about taking time off to raise children.

Gender Differences and Jobs

Another reason for the pay inequity, though, is that many teenage girls have not convinced themselves that they are capable of holding high-powered corporate jobs. That was the conclusion drawn by The Committee of 200, an organization of women executives who commissioned a 2002 study of girls' attitudes about corporate careers. The study questioned more than 3,000 teenage girls and about 1,200 teenage boys on their career goals. It found

Microsoft and technology. We have a lot of technology in our home, but I want them to see it from other people's perspectives, and to show them what is possible."

The Ms. Foundation estimated that 150 million children accompanied their parents to work in the first 20 years of the event. Marie Wilson, president of the Ms. Foundation, told the *Boston Globe* that her organization decided to expand the program to both genders because it was clear that boys and girls had similar concerns about whether they could balance the needs of their families with their career goals.

"When we started Take Our Daughters to Work Day, the focus was on careers," Wilson told the newspaper, "but we also wanted to help girls become more visible. We wanted to look at the larger lives of girls, and we found that the workplace was a good place to start. So, the program helped to teach them about the world of work. But throughout the program, girls would visit a company and their primary concern was whether they could have a family and still work there. So, that led us to ask this question, 'Can boys be family men and still work in corporate America?'"

that 15 percent of the boys and 9 percent of the girls were likely to pursue careers in business. "Boys express more interest in making lots of money, while girls are more likely to place a higher importance on helping others and making the world a better place," the study reported. "Girls made direct connections between their aspirations to help others and their preferred careers. This helps understand their affinity for careers in law and medicine."

Why were fewer girls attracted to careers in business? The Committee of 200 study said girls "see fewer positive aspects in business careers than boys. Girls perceive business careers as more stressful, less satisfying and less exciting than boys. In addition, girls tend to see business as constraining and inflexible, and not a place that is 'for them' . . . a large number of girls talked about their negative perceptions of business. This included the 'cubicle-culture,' which was also manifested as an uncreative environment where individuals are invisible and faceless."

The study suggested that girls do not have enough positive role models leading them to consider careers in business. When it comes to career advice most girls listen to their mothers rather than their fathers, the study said, even though it is usually the fathers whose jobs are more likely to be in business. Also, the study said the media rarely portray women in business as positive role models. "As part of the study, we analyzed popular TV shows, magazines, movies and websites for their content on business careers," the study said. "We found few depictions of business people. When they are present, business people tend to be male. Moreover, their jobs are vague or humorous, and peripheral to the plot line. This is in sharp contrast to shows that center on other professions such as medicine or law."

The consulting firm Arthur Andersen found similar results

when it commissioned its own study into the career aspirations of teenage girls. Arthur Andersen spokesperson Karen L. Kurek explained that her firm wanted to know why young women in the company seemed to have little interest in moving up into senior management positions. To find the answer, Arthur Andersen surveyed 500 girls and 150 boys between the ages of 15 and 18. Writing in *BW*, a publication of the organization Business and Professional Women, Kurek said, "Among the most striking findings was the fact that many of the young women, while clearly ambitious, didn't see a place for themselves in corporate America, and had a lukewarm impression of computer-related studies."

Trends may be changing, though. For example, if young people expect to follow careers into top corporate management positions, they would do well to go to college. A Gallup Youth Survey conducted in 2000 and 2001 found that 67 percent of girls and 58 percent of boys said they intended to become full-time college students following high school. In 1982, a similar poll determined that just 51 percent of girls and 40 percent of boys intended to go to college full time after high school. With more girls than boys going to college, experts believe it is only a matter of time before the pay equity gap closes even further.

Helping Girls Gain Confidence

One of the major findings of the Arthur Andersen study was that teenage girls seemed unsure of their computer skills—a major handicap if girls expect to attain high-ranking corporate positions, particularly with high-tech companies. "Interestingly," Kurek wrote, "boys were twice as likely as girls to say they would consider being a computer scientist or the CEO of a high-tech company, while girls were most interested in pursuing a career in health services and being a teacher, small business owner, or the CEO of a clothing company."

The Gallup Youth Survey has also found that girls tend to be less sure of their computer skills than boys and less interested in high-tech jobs. A 2003 Gallup Youth Survey found that computer professional was the top career choice among boys; on the girls' side, just 2 percent of the respondents said their top career choice was "scientist." And in a 2001 poll by the Gallup Youth Survey, 64 percent of the boys said they "can usually learn electronic equipment or computer software the first time without help," while 52 percent of girls felt this confident. In addition, 53 percent of boys indicated an interest in "spending more time using computers that I do," compared to 45 percent of the girls surveyed.

Many businesses and organizations have started programs to help teenage girls gain confidence in their computer skills. Arthur Andersen established a program it called MOUSE—Making Opportunities for Upgrading Schools and Education—which helps train teenage girls in information technology and makes women with high-tech careers available as mentors. The Institute of Electrical and Electronics Engineers and several other engineering-related trade groups sponsor an annual event called "Introduce a Girl to Engineering Day." More than 11,000 women engineers spend the day explaining their jobs and the technical skills they require to an estimated 1 million teenage girls. And every summer, the giant software company Microsoft sponsors DigiGirlz High Tech Camp, a three-day information technology program that gives more than 60 girls a chance to participate in tours, discussions, seminars, and hands-on training. Each day of the camp, a female Microsoft employee serves as keynote speaker and explains to the girls the opportunities they can find in high-tech careers.

Another place where teenage girls are exposed to high-tech careers is at the Sally Ride Science Camp at Stanford University in California. Each year, about 60 girls in sixth through eighth grades learn about astronomy, bioengineering, and structural engineering in the weeklong camp. Sally Ride (1951-2012), who in 1983 became the first American woman to orbit the earth, organized the camp and for many years led some of the classes. Ride once said that she had started the camp to keep young women interested in high-tech careers. Ride urged the girls to "pick an area of science you're interested in and take it as far as you can."

Studies show that girls tend to feel less confident in their computer skills than boys. In recent years a number of programs have been established to help combat this problem.

Chapter Eight

The main reason people work is to earn money, yet studies show that many young people do not understand much about the best ways to save their money.

Teens and Personal Finance

When Aaron Mallin was 18 years old, he earned $125 a week working in an ice cream store in Troy, Michigan. A lot of that money went to pay Aaron's car insurance as well as the other expenses of a typical 18-year-old. Nevertheless, each week Aaron managed to put away $30 into his savings, investing in utility stocks and a mutual fund. "I have about $3,000 invested so far, and it makes me feel secure about my future to have this," Aaron told a reporter for the *Detroit Free Press*.

Louisville, Kentucky, teenager Toni Calloway managed to save $2,000 after working as a part-time cashier and a summer job as a waitress. With that much cash in the bank, Toni said she enjoyed the feeling of never having to ask her parents for spending money. "It makes me feel more mature," she told a reporter for *USA Today*.

Studies show that quite a few teenagers manage to save some of the money they earn. In 1999, *USA*

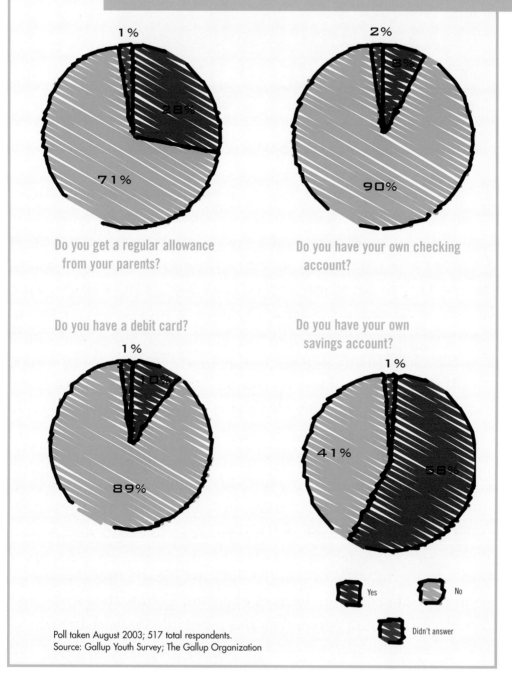

1%

28%

71%

Do you get a regular allowance from your parents?

2%

8%

90%

Do you have your own checking account?

Do you have a debit card?

Do you have your own savings account?

1%

10%

89%

1%

41%

58%

Yes   No

Didn't answer

Poll taken August 2003; 517 total respondents.
Source: Gallup Youth Survey; The Gallup Organization

Today polled nearly 200,000 teenagers on their saving and spending habits, and found that most young people do have an interest in saving and investing. Sixty-three percent of the teenagers who participated in the poll said they save money every week. "You have to think long-term," Brooke Richey, a 17-year-old student from Ridgeley, West Virginia, told the newspaper. "I know how expensive college is—and I know you have to go to college if you want to do something important. That's why, instead of going shopping every weekend, I save my money."

However, while teenagers intend to become good savers, very few of them understand much about how best to invest their money, how their investments grow, how to establish credit, how to apply for a loan for a car or a house, the importance of starting a retirement savings plan, or dozens of other matters that concern money. Few of them realize that once they graduate from high school or college and obtain full-time employment, there are many decisions they will have to make about what to do with their paychecks.

The *USA Today* survey proved that many teenagers have little comprehension about how much money they will need to survive in the economy. For example, 42 percent of the respondents said they would expect to earn $75,000 a year by the time they are 30 years old. That estimate is way off the mark. In the year *USA Today* conducted the survey, the average salary for a 30-year-old American worker was $27,000 a year.

The Gallup Youth Survey has also examined teenagers and their saving habits. In 2003, the Gallup Organization asked 517 young people between the ages of 13 and 17 how they save their money. Fifty-eight percent of the respondents said they have savings accounts. A total of 65 percent of the girls and 52 percent of the boys said they maintain interest-bearing accounts in banks.

Just 8 percent of the respondents said they have checking accounts. Usually, checking accounts do not earn interest. People use checks to pay bills, because most companies that provide goods and services would rather not handle cash. A check gives the recipient of the money permission to draw a specified amount of money from the payer's account. Ten percent of the teens responding to the Gallup Youth Survey said they have a debit card, which is similar to a check, giving the recipient electronic access to the payer's account.

Should Courses in Personal Finance Be Required?

Some experts believe high schools would do well to make personal finance a required course. In fact, a growing number of states have moved in this direction. In 2000 only three American states included personal finance classes in the curriculum schools were required to teach. By 2013, 15 states had incorporated personal finance into the curriculum.

Recent studies have shown that personal finance classes can be very effective when they are taught by properly trained teachers. A 2011 study conducted at the University of Arizona found that high school students who were given financial education showed not only an increase in knowledge of economics and finance, but also showed more responsible financial behavior when they became young adults.

In a 2012 study, Professors Rich MacDonald, Ken Rebeck, and William Walstad found that students learned roughly 20 percent more about the benefits of saving and investing when they took structured courses taught by well-trained teachers. Unfortunately, the problem is that many people teaching personal finance are not well-trained. A study conducted in 2009 at the University of Wisconsin found that less than 20 percent of teachers felt competent in teaching the personal finance concepts commonly included in educational standards. Use of poorly designed or confusing lesson plans often makes the problem worse.

Although a growing number of high schools are making personal finance courses available, American teenagers would be smart to start learning about money matters on their own.

A teacher explains how to balance a checkbook. The number of high schools that offer classes in personal finance has been growing in recent years.

Nobody expects the typical teen to start reading the *Wall Street Journal* or watch the investment experts who comment on CNBC or other financial news networks. Still, there are some steps that young people can take to learn about money.

David Gardner and Tom Gardner, founders of a syndicated financial advice newspaper column called the Motley Fool, recommend in their book *The Motley Fool Investment Guide for Teens* that young people can start by first learning how to save and spend their own money. The authors encourage teenagers to sit down and draw up a budget—calculating by the week or month how much money they expect to earn. Once teens know how much money they'll have for the month, they can decide how much to spend on entertainment or clothes, for example, and—most importantly—how much to put away in savings.

"Now that you can see where your money is coming from and going to, you might be surprised," the Gardners write. "Perhaps you didn't realize that you were spending so much of your money on gifts for others. Maybe your car is eating up a lot more money than you thought. Maybe all that snack food is packing your waistline and unpacking your wallet!"

Options for Saving

If teens have jobs, the Gardners urge them to spend some time studying their paychecks. When a teenager receives his first paycheck, he or she will undoubtedly notice that the net amount of the check is substantially less than the full value of the wages. By learning about their paychecks, teenagers can learn about state and federal taxes and Social Security payments as well as health insurance and retirement plans—all of which are typical payroll deductions.

Once teenagers understand their paychecks and establish budgets for themselves, they should spend some time exploring ways to save. The choices can be overwhelming, but the Gardners recommend young people start at the local bank or credit union, where they can investigate the types of savings programs that are available. A young person may want to consider a savings account or, if he or she expects to write checks, a checking account. There are also money-market accounts, which sometimes pay higher interest rates than savings accounts but may require a certain amount of money to be kept in the account. A certificate of deposit (CD) pays a fixed rate, but buying a CD means the saver cannot touch the money for a certain period of time, usually several months or even years. There are also bonds, issued by private companies as well as the federal government. The bonds often pay higher interest rates than savings accounts and certificates of deposit, but the money cannot be touched without penalty for a very long time—in some cases, 15, 20, or 30 years.

Those are just a few of the options available to young people with an interest in saving. There are many other ways to save money, and some are riskier than others. Although there have been many stories of people becoming rich from investing in the stock market, young people should be wary. There are more than 2,300 stocks listed on the New York Stock Exchange and another 2,700 traded in a second U.S. stock market known as the NASDAQ, which specializes in high-tech companies. There are also thousands of mutual funds in operation. These are funds in which investors pool their money to buy stocks and other investments. Most funds specialize in certain types of investments, although some have minimum investment thresholds that many teenagers would not be able to meet. Smart investors typically spend time studying a stock or a mutual fund before they invest their money, or they may seek the advice of a professional investments counselor. Most teenagers who have full social and school calendars would find themselves hard-pressed to make the time as well as find the resources to dabble in the stock market.

But some do, and are successful. One student from New York named Michael rose every morning at 6 A.M. so he could watch CNBC before leaving for school. At night, he read reports on companies' earnings and surfed the Web, looking for information on promising investments. For Michael, the early mornings and the long hours spent researching the market paid off. At the age of 9, Michael talked his parents into letting him invest $4,000. By the time he reached the age of 13, Michael was making nice profits on his investments and also giving investment advice to his 22-year-old brother as well as his parents. "When I was 10, my dad would check what I was buying for him," Michael told a reporter for *Business Week*. "But when I was $11^1/_2$, he started giving me full permission to do trades myself."

Another student, 16-year-old Bibi of Larchmont, New York, told *Business Week* that she earned $7,000 in profit after investing her own money over a four-year period. "I'm in it for the learning experience," she explained.

At the age of 8, Timothy Olsen started out with $165 to invest, which he used to buy five shares of Pepsico, the manufacturer of the soft drink Pepsi. He bought Pepsico at $33 a share; five years later, the stock was worth $47 a share, meaning he earned a profit on paper of $70. (Young investors should be aware that once Timothy sold the stock and received his profit in cash, the actual return was a bit less than $70. He owed fees to the stockbroker and had to pay taxes on his profit as well.) Timothy had an even better return when he bought 400 shares of a company named Crown Cork & Seal for $1.25 a share, then sold it a few months later at $11.75 per share. He turned an investment of $500 in Crown Cork & Seal stock into $4,200. Over the years Timothy has bought stock in airlines, railroads, energy companies, and heavy industries. His goal was to earn enough money to finance his own college education.

In recent years, the percentage of Americans who own stocks has declined significantly. In 2007, the Gallup Organization found that 65 percent of Americans owned stocks. That year, an economic recession began and stocks lost some of their value, leading people to sell and get out of the market. By 2013, although many stocks had regained their value, Gallup found that only 52 percent of Americans invested their money in the stock market.

Within six years, Timothy's savvy investing had turned his initial $165 investment into a portfolio worth $70,000. The Cranford, New Jersey, teenager became so good at investing that he wrote a book titled *The Teenage Investor: How to Start Early, Invest Often and Build Wealth.* "I wrote this book actually because I was bored and just started writing down my thoughts on investing and the general financial markets," Timothy told a reporter for the *St. Petersburg Times.* "As I wrote more and more, it became easier. I truly enjoy giving advice on investing." His advice to young investors is, "when you get money, save a lot. The earlier you start, the better."

To become such a whiz at investing, Timothy gave up some of the more typical teenage pursuits. Instead of watching entertainment or sports programming on TV, Timothy watched CNBC. Instead of playing video games, Timothy surfed the internet looking for tips on good investments. But one reason Timothy wanted to learn as much as he could about investing was because his ultimate career goal was to work on Wall Street—the financial center of the United States, where experts make big money investing billions of dollars. And his work paid off—by the time he was in his 20s Timothy was consulting for Wall Street firms and appearing on financial television shows.

Few teens can hope to match Timothy Olsen's skill in the stock market, but there is no question that like Timothy, most young people have career goals and they are doing something about meeting them. Whether they want to work on Wall Street, or they are looking into a career in the medical fields, or they are thinking about the military as an option, or they aspire to become skilled workers in the trades, today's teenagers will soon be taking their places in the working world. Many of them are getting ready. Typical, perhaps, is Malika Glover, a Kalamazoo, Michigan, student who saw her career talents blossom in her high school's school-to-work program. "At 17, not many of my friends can say, 'I have a skill,'" Malika told *Education Week*, "And that makes me kind of proud of myself."

Glossary

BONDS—certificates recognizing a debt to be repaid over a period of time to individuals, who provide money to a government or corporation. A city government may sell bonds to investors so that it can raise money to make a public improvement, such as erecting a new water treatment plant. In return, the bond holder is paid back the money he loaned as well as a guaranteed interest rate after a predetermined amount of time.

BUDGET—a plan that estimates how much money will be received and how much will be spent by an individual or organization.

ENTREPRENEUR—person who takes the initiative to start a business and make it a success.

ETHICS—behavior regarded as morally acceptable by society.

ETIQUETTE—code of conduct acceptable in social and professional situations.

INTEREST-BEARING ACCOUNT—a bank account that pays interest on deposits in exchange for allowing the bank to borrow the money for investments.

MEDIAN—in statistics, the point that equally divides two parts. A median salary would be the salary in which half the salaries are higher than the median and half lower.

MENTOR—a veteran employee who uses his or her experience and knowledge to help younger workers.

NET—the amount that is left after expenses, taxes, and other fees are deducted.

PENSION—fund established by a company or labor union to provide income to retired employees, who typically contribute part of their salaries to the fund.

PORTFOLIO—all investments owned by an individual.

Glossary

RÉSUMÉ—brief history of an individual's employment and education, usually shown to a prospective employer.

RECESSION—a period during which there is a decline in economic trade and prosperity.

SOCIAL SECURITY—a program established by the federal government in the 1930s to ensure that retirees have a guaranteed source of income. All American workers contribute to Social Security.

STOCK—share of a company traded on an exchange; an investor who owns a share of stock actually owns a piece of the company. Beliefs by investors in the success or failure of the company will cause the shares to rise or dip in value over time, thus changing the price of the stock originally paid for the shares.

STOCKBROKER—professional hired by an investor to buy and sell shares of stocks on the New York Stock Exchange and other stock markets.

Internet Resources

http://www.gallup.com

Visitors to the Internet site maintained by The Gallup Organization can find results of Gallup Youth Surveys as well as many other research projects undertaken by the national polling firm.

http://www.bls.gov

An agency of the U.S. Labor Department, the U.S. Bureau of Labor Statistics tracks the economy and issues reports on jobs, salaries, and other labor issues. Numerous reports on the state of the U.S. economy, including projections on job and wage growth, are available for down-loading or viewing on-line.

http://www.familiesandwork.org

The New York-based Families and Work Institute is a nonprofit organi-zation that studies workplace issues. Studies by the institute that focus on how labor issues affect home life are available online.

http://www.sreb.org

Students can learn more about the High Schools That Work program by visiting the Internet page of the program's sponsor, the Southern Regional Education Board based in Atlanta, Georgia. Students who participate in High Schools That Work undergo a rigorous curriculum in mathematics, sciences, and English intended to teach them skills that future employers will value.

http://www.workforceexplorer.com

The Washington state-based Workforce Explorer economic research council publishes essays and studies on economic conditions, includ-ing labor economist Paul Turke's essay "Tough Times for Teens."

Internet Resources

http://www.usma.edu

http://www.usna.edu

http://www.usafa.af.mil

Information on applying to the U.S. military service academies can be obtained at their World Wide Web sites. Students can also read histories of the academies, learn about their traditions, and gain an insight into the curriculums they offer.

http://www.strengthsquest.com

The home page for the StrengthsQuest program, developed by the Gallup Organization to help students identify their areas of greatest talent and use them for academic success and to help select the right career.

http://www.daughtersandsonstowork.org

This website for the annual Take Our Daughters and Sons to Work Day is maintained by the Ms. Foundation for Women. Visitors can find news articles written about the event in the past, research about young peoples' career choices, and statements of support for the program made by many political and corporate leaders.

http://www.fool.com/teens/teens.htm

The Motley Fool established this website specifically for teenagers and other young investors. Young people can learn how the stock market works and find information on ways to invest their money.

Further Reading

Cohen, Maria, and Douglas J. Besharov. *The Role of Career and Technical Education: Implications for the Federal Government.* Report prepared for the Office of Vocational Education, U.S. Department of Education, March 21, 2002.

Gardner, David, and Tom Gardner. *The Motley Fool Investment Guide for Teens.* New York: Simon and Schuster, 2002.

Llewelly, A. Bronwyn, and Robin Holt. *The Everything Career Tests Book: Ten Tests to Determine the Right Occupation for You.* Avon, Mass.: Adams Media, 2007.

Lore, Nicholas. *Now What? The Young Person's Guide to Choosing the Perfect Career.* New York: Fireside, 2008.

Mamlet, Robin, and Christine Vandevelde. *College Admission: From Application to Acceptance, Step by Step.* New York: Three Rivers Press, 2011.

Olsen, Timothy. *The Teenage Investor.* New York: McGraw-Hill, 2003.

Pierce, Valerie, and Cheryl Rilly. *Countdown to College: 21 To Do List for High School.* Bath, Mich.: Front Porch Press, 2009.

Shatkin, Laurence. *Quick Guide to College Majors and Careers.* Indianapolis: JIST Publishing Inc., 2002.

Silverberg, Marsha, Elizabeth Warner, David Goodwin, and Michael Fong. *National Assessment of Vocational Education: Interim Report to Congress.* Report prepared for the Office of the Undersecretary, U.S. Education Department, 2002.

Teens Guide to College and Career Planning. 11th ed. Lawrenceville, N.J.: Peterson's Publishing, 2011.

Vanderberg, Tom, ed. *The College Board Index to Majors and Graduate Degrees.* New York: The College Board, 2003.

Index

Numbers in **bold italic** refer to captions and graphs.

Index

Index

Index

Picture Credits

Contributors

GEORGE GALLUP JR. (1930–2011) was involved with The Gallup Organization for more than 50 years. He served as chairman of The George H. Gallup International Institute and served on many boards involved with health, education, and religion, including the Princeton Religion Research Center, which he co-founded.

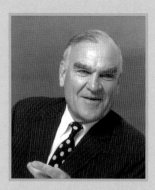

Mr. Gallup was internationally recognized for his research and study on youth, health, religion, and urban problems. He wrote numerous books, including *My Kids On Drugs?* with Art Linkletter (Standard, 1981); *The Great American Success Story* with Alec Gallup and William Proctor (Dow Jones-Irwin, 1986); *Growing Up Scared in America* with Wendy Plump (Morehouse, 1995); *Surveying the Religious Landscape: Trends in U.S. Beliefs* with D. Michael Lindsay (Morehouse, 1999); and *The Next American Spirituality* with Timothy Jones (Chariot Victor Publishing, 2002).

Mr. Gallup received his BA degree from the Princeton University Department of Religion in 1954, and held seven honorary degrees. He received many awards, including the Charles E. Wilson Award in 1994, the Judge Issacs Lifetime Achievement Award in 1996, and the Bethune-DuBois Institute Award in 2000. Mr. Gallup passed away in November 2011.

THE GALLUP YOUTH SURVEY was founded in 1977 by Dr. George Gallup to provide ongoing information on the opinions, beliefs and activities of America's high school students and to help society meet its responsibility to youth. The topics examined by the Gallup Youth Survey have covered a wide range — from abortion to zoology. From its founding through the year 2001, the Gallup Youth Survey sent more than 1,200 weekly reports to the Associated Press, to be distributed to newspapers around the nation.

HAL MARCOVITZ is a Pennsylvania-based journalist. He has written more than 50 books for young readers. His other titles for the Gallup Youth Survey series include *Teens and Career Choices* and *Teens and Volunteerism*. He lives in Chalfont, Pennsylvania, with his wife, Gail, and daughters Ashley and Michelle.